Norman Macleod's

Trout Fishing in Lewis

Roddy J Macleod
Eddie Young

© 1977, 1985, 1993 — All enquiries to the publisher please

Western Isles Publishing Co Ltd
Stornoway Business Centre

Printed by Essprint Ltd

ISBN 0 906437 15 6

NORMAN MACLEOD

1915 — 1984

Norman Macleod was born in the village of Coll and as a teenager moved to Stornoway where he attended The Nicolson Institute. After an apprenticeship served in the famous shipyard of John Brown and war service in the Merchant Navy he returned to his native island where he set up in business as a partner in a firm of electrical contractors. With the establishment of a shop specialising in electrical and sports goods in the early fifties, the 'Sports Shop' as it has been known to generations of Stornowegians was born.

The author's first-hand knowledge of the lochs he describes so well was based on his lifelong passsion for angling. Not content with leaning back on this knowledge, he fished every loch he mentioned during the two years he spent compiling his material. Such a meticulous approach to a job to be done was characteristic of the man.

His other interests were reflected by his long association with Stornoway Athletic Football Club, Stornoway Golf Club, Stornoway Angling Association and, latterly, Stornoway Sea Angling Club, where during his years as Chairman of the Club he played an important part in its development.

Freshwater angling, however, was his first love and remained so. In the angling boom in the sixties and seventies local and visiting anglers benefited greatly from his advice and experience, and the capturing of them in the pages of this book serves both to answer innumerable questions, and to provide us with a memorial to a brother angler.

AUTHOR'S PREFACE
to the first edition

My thanks are due to Edward Young and Roddy John MacLeod for reading the manuscript and making various corrections and suggestions, and for their enthusiastic support during the final stages of the production of this book.

I also wish to thank Colin Tucker for the cartography, and Alex Urquhart, that well-known local angler, for writing the foreword.

Anglers should be grateful to all owners of the lochs mentioned in this book, who over the years have raised no objections to the angling public fishing these waters.

There are many more lochs on the island which the enterprising angler could fish with perhaps surprising results.

There are others which may be used by the owners or their guests and should not be fished without previous enquiry or knowledge that there are no objections to fishing them.

Stornoway
July 1977

Norman Macleod

Map of Lewis showing by broken lines the geographical divisions arbitrarily chosen for this book and where to find the relevant text

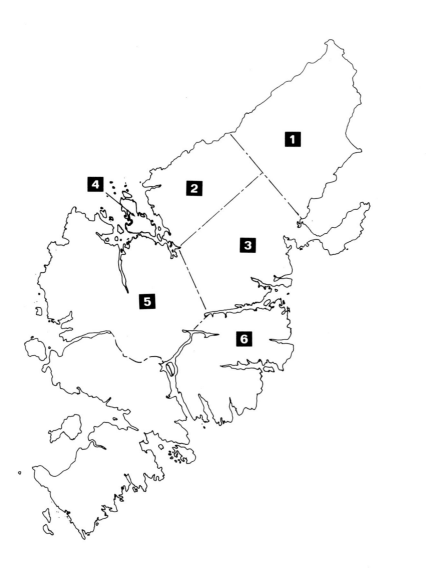

Placenames are given primarily
as they appear in Ordnance Survey maps
of the 1:50,000 Landranger Series both in the text
and in the index of lochs thereafter.

FOREWORD
to the first edition

Here, at last, is supplied a long-felt want, information on local angling facilities compiled by an expert of long personal experience. Mr Macleod is no purist; his booklet is for everyone — the fly-fisher, the spinner, the wormer. The visitor especially, scanning a map which seems to be mainly water, and with limited time at his disposal, will find it invaluable. Even the local angler with his own favourite loch may be tempted with profit further afield. Not only is it a practical comprehensive guide for beginners and visitors wondering where to go, but also for the veterans who fancy a change of scene.

With over fifty years of trudging Lewis moors and fishing Lewis lochs I can confirm much of Mr Macleod's information; it is dependable and not based on hearsay. There is an abundance of trout fishing; in many lochs too many fish for the food supply; hence the need for selection. Mr Macleod in his business has always been most helpful with freely offered reliable information, and now that this has been incorporated in booklet form he has put present and future anglers in his debt and they can fare forth with a confidence in 'tighter lines' based on secure knowledge. May it have the success it and its compiler deserve.

Stornoway   *A Urquhart*
July 1977

'An moch gu loch, moch gu abhainn, is meadhon-latha gu allt.'

'Late to the loch, early to the river, and midday to the burn'

INTRODUCTION
to the first edition

This guide to brown trout fishing in Lewis is offered in the hope that it will enable the visiting angler to choose a few lochs where he can fish and be sure that there are trout on the waters he is fishing. There are in fact very few lochs on the island which do not hold brown trout. Some are overstocked and contain small trout of only a few ounces; others have fish up to several pounds. In between are the lochs with trout of 8 oz to 1 lb.

The Island of Lewis, known to many as 'Eilean an Fhraoich' (the Isle of the Heather), could well be called the isle of a thousand lochs. In fact it contains more. There are over seven hundred lochs varying in size from five acres to three and a half square miles, and more than four hundred of lesser size. It is of course impossible for a publication of this nature to cover all of them. It would take one angler fishing one loch per day for six days a week during the season more than six years to fish them all. This is a tremendous amount of fishing water in an island approximately forty miles in length and twenty-six miles wide.

There is plenty of scope for the angler who wishes to combine moor-trekking and hill-climbing with angling. He could very well be fishing in a loch which has not been fished for years — who knows what size of trout might be lurking therein. It is in some of these rarely visited small lochs that big ones are sometimes taken and the peace and quiet provide a refreshing contrast to the roadside loch.

The vast majority of brown trout lochs on the island are free to local and visiting anglers alike, but some estate owners reserve waters for themselves and their guests. Before setting out for a day's fishing enquiries should be made locally.

The season opens on 15th March and closes on 6th October. It is very seldom that one can get trout in good condition before the middle of April. The best months for fly fishing are from the end of April until the end of June and again during the first fortnight in September. July and August are not just so good with fly, and bait or spinner may prove more productive.

Though Sunday fishing for brown trout is legal in Scotland, it would most certainly be looked upon with disfavour in Lewis and no local angler fishes on that day. It is expected that the visiting angler will respect local custom.

It is hoped that all anglers will respect the rights of the owners of the various estates, that no litter will be left behind by the lochside and that no discarded nylon will be left whether by the waterside or on the moor. Entanglement in lengths of nylon presents a hazard both to birds and to young lambs.

EDITORS' FOREWORD

Our foreword to the second edition mourned the passing of the author, Norman Macleod, and the writer of the foreword to the first edition, Alex Urquhart. As joint-editors, we are conscious of building on the sound foundations laid by Norman in the first edition in our attempts to do what he would have strongly approved of, developing the book in response to the changing conditions of our waters and the discovery of new lochs opened up by anglers following on his footsteps. To these anglers who, in the true spirit of Norman Macleod, have given so freely and generously of their experience towards the production of this book we offer our sincere gratitude. Their identities are revealed in the acknowledgements later.

Both Norman and Alex would have nodded their approval of this practical application of the motto of their own great old school, The Nicolson Institute, Stornoway: *Sequamur* — 'Let us follow'.

TACKLE, CLOTHING, EQUIPMENT, TACTICS

The following is simply a guide: anglers have their own preferences, and there is no reason why you should not follow them, but you may find this section helpful, especially if you are a visitor.

FLY

Perhaps the most generally useful all-round rod is a carbon fibre 10-footer, around AFTM 6-7, long enough to help keep your cast clear of some of the high banks round our lochs and a suitable length for boat fishing (though specialist boat fishers may prefer something longer). Match this with a trout reel holding a forward taper 7 line (floating or neutral density) for bank fishing, especially in a wind. You may wish to use lighter lines, particularly in boat fishing (when a double taper is often preferred), and especially in high summer when finer leaders and smaller flies are often necessary. In general, use the longest leader you can manage for the conditions — at least 12 feet normally, of 4 to 5 lbs breaking strain — consisting of a tail fly and, traditionally, one or two droppers. Our lochs tend to be windswept, and nylon under 5 lbs tends to tangle very easily, but always be ready to go lighter if the breeze drops.

The dry fly can work well from boat or bank either as a single fly or as part of a team, and a daddy long-legs artificial is worth trying as the natural insect is a common sight throughout the Lewis summer. Remember the dapping rod. You will rise plenty of trout: hooking them is another matter.

Do not be tempted to give up in flat calms. Nymphing tactics can work well, especially the small (often tiny) weighted fly or nymph on a long fine leader, slowly inched back. Brown trout tend to be territorial and have to be searched for. When bank fishing, the traditional cast — take a step — cast again method covers a lot of water and gives you every chance of finding fish. Staying in one spot all the time seldom works with wild brown trout. A fairly bushy bob fly such as the Black or Blue Zulu can bring up the fish, especially in a breeze, but use smaller and slimmer patterns in low wind conditions. Fan out your casts, searching the water, and make your first cast from well back as trout are often found close to the bank. If you see a rise, cover it as quickly as possible, for a rising fish is usually a taking fish.

The traditional Scottish wet flies for loch fishing are usually dependable — Silver Butcher, Peter Ross, Black Pennell, Invicta, March Brown, Alexandra, Grouse and Claret, Greenwell's Glory, the Teal series and the Worm Fly. The Welsh Coch a bonddu and Haul a Gwynt (Sun and Wind) and the Irish Claret and Golden Olive Bumbles are firmly recommended. Other excellent flies are the Black and Peacock Spider, Brown and Peacock Spider, Kate McLaren, Wickham's Fancy and the Clan Chief. There is a strong preference for small black, or at least dark, flies. But be experimental, falling back on the traditional patterns as a safety net. Sunk line tactics with large lures in the deeper lochs have scarcely been tried, but you will have most fun by drift fishing from the boat or keeping mobile on the bank.

Fly size is variable. Early in the season 10s are preferred, but 12s are the most generally useful, dropping to 14s, 16s or even 18s in difficult conditions. Use size 8 in a big blow or as a tail fly for taking your leader down. But, as ever, when all else fails try something outrageously big. The Ombudsman on a long-shank 10 is splendid in early season on a short leader fished cross-wind on a lee shore, as a point fly for loch fishing, and for any occasion throughout the season when the flies have to be taken down. It is almost certainly taken for a dragonfly nymph, and our dragonflies are very big indeed, the troop-carrying helicopters of the insect world! If you tie your own flies, as all anglers should, you will have increased opportunities to try out both old and new patterns in the ever-changing conditions you will face on our lochs.

SPINNING AND BAIT FISHING

These methods are used extensively throughout the island and produce good results. A seven-foot rod with fixed spool reel and monofilament lines of four to six pounds breaking strain are used for spinning. Lures of the Toby and Mepps type are the most popular; the revolving type such as the Devon is seldom used, but may be just as effective.

For bait fishing, heavier lines of up to ten pounds breaking strain are sometimes used, with lead weights attached for extra distance. The heavier line reduces breakages from a mistimed cast or becoming stuck on the bottom.

An increasing number of anglers, however, feel that fly fishing is a more rewarding and enjoyable method. The bait and spinning enthusiasts would increase their enjoyment if they added fly fishing to their repertoire.

CLOTHING AND EQUIPMENT

The Lewis moor can be a wild as well as a beautiful place, and it makes sense to be properly equipped for it. You will need wellington boots with a good tread, worn over warm wool socks, to give you safe and dry footing. Waders are unnecessary though useful occasionally in some lochs where the trout are lying beyond an area of shallows, but don't wear them for long treks.

A waterproof hooded jacket, preferably three-quarter length or extendable to that — and if it is made of one of the modern lightweight, breathable fabrics so much the better — will give you a water-and-wind-proof shell under which you can wear warm pullovers to be removed if the sun shines. A fishing waistcoat with a large bellows pocket to take your jacket is ideal for distributing weight during a long day's fishing.

If you intend to be out on the moor all day, a small rucksack will carry the necessary food (you can get very hungry on a windswept moor) with possibly a small portable camping stove for brewing up. Always carry the relevant Ordnance Survey map, a compass and a whistle, especially if you are out on your own, and leave word behind where you are going and when you expect to be back. The Lewis moor can be featureless in places, and a thick sea-fog can move inland without any warning. If you are boat-fishing always wear a buoyancy aid and never stand up in a boat, no matter what the practice is elsewhere. There is seldom another boat on the same loch as you, and if you fall in your chance of being rescued is very small. (In any case, standing up simply lets the trout see you better, and they then move further off!)

The Lewis midge is, by repute, not quite as bad as its relatives in Skye and the Western Highlands, but it does try hard, especially when the wind drops in the evening. Always carry a reliable anti-midge preparation. Better still, use it in conjunction with an anti-midge face net, but remember to remove it when you arrive back on the road — you don't want to be mistaken for our first Hebridean bank robber.

So equipped, you can wander, or float, safely and comfortably, often fishing lochs which may be seldom, if ever, visited by another angler, enjoying the peace and solitude of one of the last remaining wilderness areas of Europe.

SALMON AND SEATROUT

These do not come under the scope of this book, but for those who wish to fish for them, permits are available from various sources. As the details change from year to year, it is best to check with the Western Isles Tourist Board, Stornoway (Tel 0851 703088) who publish a leaflet, 'Ag Iasgach — Angling in the Western Isles', and look for the adverts in the angling press. You are strongly advised to book well in advance, though it is sometimes possible to arrange a day at short notice.

Visitors need not bring 'salmon' tackle. A single-handed, ten to eleven foot trout rod of AFTM 6-8 is perfectly adequate for loch fishing for our summer salmon (which average around six pounds) — and a great deal easier to use. Most traditional trout fly patterns in size 8 will take salmon, but by all means use your favourite salmon flies, though generally in small sizes, 10 to 8, with a few bigger ones in reserve, fished on leaders of 8-10lbs BS.

SAFETY

Anglers should take care where there are high-voltage cables overhead. Remember that a carbon fibre rod conducts electricity easily. Carry your rod low when passing under cables and never fish near them.

Please do not park in the passing places on single-track roads. If you drive along peat roads, ensure that your parked car is not blocking the way for others, especially crofters and their tractors.

When boat-fishing, follow the advice given in the section on Clothing and Equipment.

Roddy J Macleod

Stornoway
April 1993

Eddie Young

THE NORTH

This section covers the whole area of the north end of Lewis including both west and east coasts. As the terrain is mainly low-lying and landmarks are few, the wandering angler should heed the advice given earlier under Clothing and Equipment when tackling the more remote waters.

LOCH NAN LEAC

Location:	**Four and a half miles due east of the junction of the A857 (Stornoway — Ness) and A858 roads near the village of Lower Barvas.**
Grid Reference:	**430485**
Area:	**32 acres (13 hectares)**

This loch is just over three miles from the nearest road point, and the best place to set off from is the bridge at the stream called Cliastul more than half way between Stornoway and Barvas on the A857 road.

It would be advisable to take a compass on the journey since the moor is featureless and it is easy to lose one's way, especially if doing the crossing for the first time. If fog or mist come down then a compass is absolutely necessary to be sure of getting back to the road.

The water of this loch is crystal clear, unusually so for a Lewis loch, and sometimes, if you make a noise on approaching, you may see trout moving out from the shallows to deeper water.

The trout average one pound plus, and some in the two and three pounds class are frequently taken. More fish are taken on bait than on fly, but if you cast a long line fly is also productive.

The best part is the south-east corner near the remains of old shielings, and you must cast out as far as possible as it is here that the trout seem to congregate.

It fishes best with a south or south-east wind during the months of May, June, July and September. From the end of July onwards a large area of the loch is covered with green algae and is more difficult to fish.

Loch na Faing

This lies fifteen minutes walk to the north-west of Loch nan Leac. It is a round-shaped loch of attractive appearance with its light-coloured sandy bay on the north shore, rocky sides elsewhere and a small island near the south-west corner. It does not, however, fish well to the fly. It has not lived up to its earlier good reputation recently, but this may be temporary.

LOCH GRESS (GRIAIS)

Location: **The best approach is from the A857 Stornoway to Barvas road, as for Loch nan Leac.**
Grid Reference: **448502**
Area: **52 acres (21 hectares)**

This loch is at the headwaters of the Gress River, six miles upstream from the estuary. The water is clear over a mainly stony bottom; the flat stone slabs make wading somewhat difficult but the fly fisher will be able to cast into ample depth from close to the bank. The trout are plentiful, mainly between four and six ounces, rise well to the fly and fight hard.

LOCH FOISNAVAT

Location: **Lies about one mile west-north-west of Loch Gress by a fifteen minutes walk westwards, slightly uphill to a summit from where there is a distant view of a considerable length of the north-west coastline of Lewis.**
Grid Reference: **430505**
Area: **37 acres (15 hectares)**

The stone and soft mud of this loch shelve very gradually. Trout averaging eight ounces rise to the natural but do not come so readily to the artificial fly as those of Loch Gress. There are eleven fairly well preserved shielings around the loch where in the past the crofters of Shader had their summer grazings.

LOCH GUNNA

Location: **Easily accessible just over a quarter of a mile east of the A857 Stornoway to Barvas road, about five miles from Stornoway.**

Grid Reference: **405415**

Area: **22 acres (9 hectares)**

The bottom is rocky at the north shore and muddy and rocky at the south. The trout are mainly small, up to six ounces, but take the fly well. A good beginners loch.

LOCH A' GHAINMHICH

Location: **About a mile north-east of Loch Gunna.**

Grid Reference: **420427**

Area: **27 acres (11 hectares)**

An attractive loch of clear water over reddish pebbles, but weedy at its west end. It lies on an east-west axis in a shallow valley and can be easily missed. The trout are small but active and rise well to the fly.

LOCH AN TUIM

Location: **North-east of Loch a' Ghainmhich. However, it is best approached by walking east up the north side of the Roundogro River from a point at GR 395429 on the A857 Stornoway to Barvas road, the best starting point for several lochs in the area.**

Grid Reference: **425435**

Area: **25 acres (10 hectares)**

The trout are mainly under eight ounces but rise fairly freely to the fly in June and July. There are several smaller lochs immediately to the east of Loch an Tuim which contain a similar size of trout.

LOCHAN A' SGEIL

Location: **On Coll moor to the west of Loch an Eilein.**
Grid Reference: **434435**
Area: **27 acres (11 hectares)**

The loch can be approached either from the A857 Stornoway-Barvas road or by one of the peat roads beyond the village of Coll.

Most of this loch has high, peaty banks but the water is very clear. The outgoing stream has silted up, causing the water level to be higher than it was in years gone by when the loch had a clean, gravelly shore in parts.

The trout are big — some up to three and a half pounds have been taken and bigger ones have been seen. Bait or spinner is best, and the bigger ones never rise to the fly.

Best months are June, August and September and a strong breeze is necessary.

Loch Fada Caol is a quarter mile to the north of Lochan a' Sgeil. The trout are mostly similar to Loch an Tuim, but the occasional bigger one, up to three quarters of a pound, is taken. Good sport with fly in June.

LOCH AN TOBAIR

Location: **North of Loch Fada Caol.**
Grid Reference: **435455**
Area: **54 acres (22 hectares)**

Access is not easy owing to distance and the nature of the moor, and the loch is seldom fished, but good reports come from those who give it a visit.

The water is very clear and most of the trout are silvery in colour, mostly half to three-quarters of a pound, but some up to one and a half pounds have been taken.

A number of small lochs including **Loch na Fola** and **Loch nan Leac**, a short distance to the east of Loch an Tobair, also give good results, but again there is the difficulty with distance and terrain.

LOCH ULLAVAT A' DEAS and
LOCH ULLAVAT A' CLITH (CLI)

Location:	**To the south of Gress River and north-west from the village of Back.**
Grid Reference:	**455435**
Area:	**54 acres (22 hectares)**

Access to these two lochs is through the village of Back and along the peat road nearest Gress River.

Trout are fewer, though larger (average eight to ten ounces) in Loch Ullavat a' Deas. Fishing close in, on the drop-off, with small dark flies (12-14) seems most productive, particularly in southerly winds. All areas of the loch fish well but there is a definite hot-spot at the north-west point of the loch.

Fish take even in a flat calm if a single weighted small fly (down to 18 if necessary) is fished on a long fine leader of 3lbs (maximum) breaking strain.

At Loch Ullavat a' Clith trout are smaller (six to eight ounces, with some up to twelve ounces) but extremely plentiful. A good day should produce a dozen quality fish. Again, all areas of the loch are productive but the best shores, winds permitting, are the south and west ones. This loch fishes best in a strong breeze, but in a calm the fine-and-far-off tactics as suggested for the sister loch should produce a basket. Generally, however, bigger flies work well on this loch, with size 10 recommended in a wave and 12s and 14s in lower winds. Again, dark flies work well, especially Black and Peacock Spider, Black Pennell, Mallard and Claret, Sooty Olive and March Brown.

LOCH AN EILEIN

Location:	**West of Loch Ullavat a' Clith.**
Grid Reference:	**445435**
Area:	**25 acres (10 hectares)**

Head waters of the Coll River, with access either from the peat roads at Back or Coll. Small trout only, but plentiful. Sea trout get up here after a heavy spate, from the end of June onwards, and some salmon are taken during August, September and October.

It is also worthwhile fishing the Coll River when in spate because as well as brown trout there is always the chance of sea trout and salmon.

LOCH BACAVAT

Location: **Half-way between the village of Gress and Glen Tolsta to the west of the main road.**
Grid Reference: **502442**
Area: **12 acres (5 hectares)**

Five minutes walk from, though not in sight of, the main road, this is a pleasant loch for an evening's fishing.

Trout vary in size from six ounces to three-quarters of a pound and it fishes best during June and September, but it can of course be fished during the whole season. Best parts are the south side, east and west of the outgoing stream, and the whole of the northern shore.

LOCH SGEIREACH MOR

Location: **Due west of Glen Tolsta.**
Grid Reference: **490455**
Area: **37 acres (15 hectares)**

Not to be confused with Loch Mor Sgeireach one mile to the north. The trout, though not big, are plentiful, and give good sport with a westerly breeze.

Best approached from Allt Raonadale (a stream between Gress and Glen Tolsta). Keeping to the north end of Loch Corrasavat, head towards the south and west sides of the loch as the ground to the east is marshy.

LOCH NAN GEADH

Location: **Half a mile north-west of Loch Sgeireach Mor.**
Grid Reference: **484464**
Area: **15 acres (6 hectares)**

If you venture as far as Loch Sgeireach Mor, Loch nan Geadh is within easy reach and is worth a visit. The trout average half a pound with the occasional three-quarter pounder.

Ten minutes walk north-west from here there is a small loch **(GR 481468)**, unnamed on the map. Though dour this loch can sometimes give good results with a stiff south-westerly wind. Trout over three pounds have been taken here.

LOCH MOR A' GHOBA (GHOBHA)

Location: **Due north from Loch nan Geadh.**
Grid Reference: **485472**
Area: **20 acres (8 hectares)**

This loch is over two miles from the bridge at Glen Tolsta. The trout vary from six to ten ounces and it fishes best during June, July and September. It is on higher ground than most of the Lewis lochs, being four hundred feet above sea level.

From Glen Tolsta Bridge the easiest route is towards the south end of **Loch Ionadagro** which has an abundance of small sized trout.

Northwest from Loch Ionadagro there is a small **unnamed loch** (GR 501468) from which trout varying in size between one pound and three and a quarter pounds have been taken with bait and spinner, but they never rise to fly.

There are numerous other small lochs in this area all containing trout of varying size, and all well worth spending some time on.

LOCH SCARRASDALE (SGARRASDAIL)

Location: **Head waters of the Garry River.**
Grid Reference: **503498**
Area: **20 acres (8 hectares)**

The trout here are mostly under half a pound and are not in very good condition until June. After a heavy spate, from July onwards, salmon and sea trout which have made their way up the Garry River enter the loch. During September and October they go as far as Loch Nic Dhomhnuill and Loch Vatacolla at the base of Muirneag.

The loch is shallow and most of it, especially the east shore, can be waded. It is here and at the south shore that the fish usually lie.

Access is by following the Garry River, which has a few pools which can be fished if the water level is high enough.

A shorter route is to follow the peat road to the left at the north end of North Tolsta. With care this can be done by car, and will take you to the east end of Loch Diridean. From here onwards, it is rough moorland, boggy in parts during wet weather.

LOCH NA CLOICH

Location: **To the south of Loch Scarrasdale.**
Grid Reference: **508490**
Area: **37 acres (15 hectares)**

A stony loch and not very interesting. Small trout of six ounces and under are plentiful. The east side, which is the best part, sometimes yields the odd half-pounder.

Access is by the same peat road to **Loch Diridean** where the trout are similar in size.

LOCH BEAG EILEAVAT and
LOCH MOR EILEAVAT

Location: **Three and a half miles north-west of the village of North Tolsta.**
Grid Reference: **511540**
Area: **60 acres (24 hectares)**

For anyone prepared for more than an hour's walk, this brace of lochs known as the Eileavats is well worth a visit.

Loch Beag Eileavat, which is the better of the two, is actually two lochs connected by a very short stream. The eastern arm of the loch is perhaps the better as far as weight is concerned, and trout of two pounds and over are sometimes taken here though the average weight is three-quarters of a pound. The western arm, or north-south section, holds trout of a smaller size but more plentiful and with a favourable westerly breeze is very good for fly fishing. If conditions are not suitable, spinner or bait is more productive.

On Loch Mor Eileavat, a short distance to the south, trout are mostly under half a pound but give good sport.

The lochs fish best during June, the first half of July and in September, but fish can of course be taken during the whole season.

The starting-off point for these lochs is Amhuinn na Cloich, GR 535510, which is about a half mile to the north of Abhainn Geiraha (Garry River) at North Tolsta. From Garry Bridge to Amhuinn na Cloich is not very suitable for motoring though people do take their cars. Care must be taken however as the surface is very rough.

From here head north-west between Loch Fuaimavat and Loch Eillagval. There is a gentle rise from two hundred feet above sea level to four hundred feet.

LOCHAN VATALEOIS

Location: **To the east and south-east of the Eileavats.**
Grid Reference: **518538**
Area: **35 acres (14 hectares)**

This the largest and best of a group of five lochs is nearest the Eileavats, and has  the remains of old shielings at its north and east sides.

Trout of six to ten ounces are plentiful and bank fishing is possible round the whole of its perimeter though the east side is stony and not easily waded.

The starting-off point is the same as for the Eileavats.

LOCH LANGAVAT

Location: **North-east of the Vataleois group.**
Grid Reference: **525545**
Area: **153 acres (62 hectares)**

This loch, within easy walking distance of the previous lochs, is over one mile long. Not a very interesting loch to fish. Trout are small but plentiful.

LOCH SGEIREACH NA CREIGE BRIST

Location: **Near the coast, to the east of Loch Langavat.**
Grid Reference: **545535**
Area: **25 acres (10 hectares)**

This clear-water loch, situated less than quarter of a mile from the high cliffs of the east coast, has in the last few years produced trout from three to over five pounds but all were taken on bait or spinner.

Some years ago this was a very good fly fishing loch when baskets of three quarters to one and a half pounds were common, but now most reports are of a bigger class of good quality trout which unfortunately are not always in a taking mood.

Nevertheless, this loch is well worth a visit by any angler in search of a big one, who does not mind the walk. If unsuccessful there are other lochs in the vicinity and on the way back which can be fished.

Again the starting-off point is from Amhuinn na Cloich, keeping to the east of Loch Caol Duin Othail and the two small lochs lying to the north of it. Do not keep close to the coast as the moor here is rather difficult to walk.

In addition to the lochs already mentioned, in this area north of the River Garry, from easting forty-nine eastwards towards the coast, there are thirty other lochs varying in size from five to thirty-six acres, all of which can give good sport with trout mostly from six to eight ounces.

North-west and a short distance from Loch Eillagval (GR 528525) and to the east of a triangle-shaped loch there is a small narrow loch **(GR 525528)** — both lochs are unnamed on the map. The trout on this small loch are up to two and a half pounds but seldom rise to the fly and are usually taken on bait or spinner.

West of Loch Beag Sandavat and Loch Mor Sandavat (GR 500525) there are numerous very small lochs of which any can produce a surprise for the angler prepared to explore this area of the moor. Some good fish have been taken here, but the area is seldom fished.

LOCH DIBADALE (DIBEADAIL)

Location:	**Just west of the village of South Dell.**
Grid Reference:	**480613**
Area:	**12 acres (5 hectares)**

Easily accessible, only 400 yards off the main A857 Stornoway to Ness road at the first turning left after the cattle grid.

This very shallow loch with good access and easy casting was restocked some years ago. Trout reputed to be up to three pounds have been seen rising on summer evenings. Surprisingly, it is little fished, and the persevering angler may receive a pleasant surprise. Adjacent reseeding has improved the loch.

Wading and long casting are necessary because of the shallow nature of the loch. The best side is the south, and fishing with dark flies in sizes 12 and 14 is recommended. April, May and June are best, after which algal blooms make fishing difficult.

LOCH BARAVAT

Location:	**Immediately adjacent to the A857 Stornoway to Ness road, north-east of Galson Lodge.**
Grid Reference:	**462596**
Area:	**5 acres (2 hectares)**

A small lochan very close to the main road but known to have produced fish in the five to six pounds class in recent years. There are good rises on a calm spring or summer evening near the small island and causeway.

Small flies (14-16) on long fine leaders should produce trout of ten to twelve ounces, but be prepared for something much bigger!

Late evenings in May, June and September are best.

LOCH CHEARASAIDH

Location: **Park at Galson Lodge on the A857 Stornoway to Ness road. Follow the Galson River for about 20 minutes. The loch can be seen to your left.**

Grid Reference: **467582**

Area: **2.5 acres (1 hectare)**

Another small lochan, boggy in early season but not dangerously so. Very good head of sizeable trout, average twelve ounces, but recently a bag of six weighing five pounds has been taken on fly.

Size 10 and 12 dark flies fished close in from well back is a proven tactic, as are long casts to the centre of the lochan. All sides fish well, but the southern shore is strongly recommended.

LOCH RUISAVAT

Location: **Park at Galson Lodge on the A857 Stornoway to Ness road. Follow the Galson River upstream for about an hour to the shielings. The loch is on your right but hard to see in the hollow.**

Grid Reference: **482568**

Area: **10 acres (4 hectares)**

Locally, this loch has a big reputation though recent reports suggest a deterioration in both quality and quantity of fish. Bags of 12 trout in the ten to twelve ounce class were common in recent years. The loch is now underfished and is worth trying with a team of dark flies in sizes 10 and 12, especially close to the south shore over the drop-off; so wading is unnecessary.

LOCH RUMSAGRO

Location: **Take the peat road opposite the public phone box in South Galson on the A857 Stornoway to Ness Road. Park at the water tower. Follow pipeline to Loch Striamavat (small fish) then swing east-north-east to Loch Rumsagro. The whole walk takes about 50 minutes.**

Grid Reference: **463558**

Area: **15 acres (6 hectares)**

Fish in the six to seven-ounce class fairly plentiful. Small dark flies and south shore recommended.

LOCH RUIGLAVAT

Location:	Proceed as for Loch Rumsagro. Loch Ruiglavat is a ten-minute walk south-east of Loch Rumsagro.
Grid Reference:	467557
Area:	10 acres (4 hectares)

1

An excellent loch with fish averaging twelve ounces, but there are much bigger fish for the taking. A nine-year-old angler landed trout of one and a quarter and one and a half pounds recently.

Fish alongside the weeded areas. The best fishing is around the bay on the south-east where you should fish the drop-off close to the bank. The north-west shore fishes well but requires longer casting. Beware the boggy area and steep banks on the north side.

Bumbles and Hardy's Favourite in sizes 10 and 12 are strongly recommended.

LOCH LEISAVAT

Location:	Take the peat road opposite the public phone box in South Galson on the A857 Stornoway to Ness road. Park at the end of the track. Head south-west over easy moorland for about fifteen minutes.
Grid Reference:	435571
Area:	5 acres (2 hectares)

Wading not recommended as the loch is deep inshore. Fish from well back first (always good practice) before casting out into the loch. Dark patterns in 10, 12 and 14 according to wind are recommended.

Good average size (ten to twelve ounces) with some over the pound. Savage takes and boisterous fights the norm!

Very good loch for dry fly tactics (sedges, hoppers, mini-muddlers, etc) on calm sunny days or late evenings.

All areas fish well, especially in a southerly wind, but south side recommended.

As this is a seagull nursery be prepared to be buzzed by irate parents!

LOCH BACAVAT

Location:	**Immediately to the west of the A857 Stornoway to Ness road just north of Shader.**
Grid Reference:	**398552**
Area:	**6 acres (2.5 hectares)**

A small lochan, handy for an evening's fishing, with a very heavy stock of six to twelve-ounce fish. Despite its proximity to the road it is seriously underfished and there can be impressive rises in the calm conditions of late evening when a team of small flies (14-16) on a fine leader could bring a pleasant surprise.

Best in April, May and June, after which heavy weed growth develops.

LOCH AN DUIN

Location:	**Adjacent to main A857 road in Shader. Follow peat road round south end of loch and park at the monument.**
Grid Reference:	**394543**
Area:	**25 acres (10 hectares)**

Very rich water which holds a considerable head of free-rising trout and which fishes well all season, though best in April to June.

Small flies and light tippets recommended. Dry fly and nymph techniques work well. Waders are useful as loch is shallow to well out, but be careful of rocks and patches of soft peat.

Best part is from the Dun to the south bay where a bag of eight to twelve good trout can reasonably be expected.

LOCH MARAVAT

Location:	**Take the peat road at the north end of Loch an Duin adjacent to the main A857 road in the village of Shader. Park at the end of the track. The loch is a five-minute walk to the south-east.**
Grid Reference:	**404536**
Area:	**25 acres (10 hectares)**

Very good trout averaging twelve ounces. Fishes well in all areas but best from April to June and then September.

LOCH KEARTAVAT (CEARTAVAT)

Location: **Take the peat road at south end of Loch an Duin, Shader, parking at the end of the track. A twenty-minute walk to the south-east over reasonable moor will bring you to the loch.**
Grid Reference: **417523**
Area: **32 acres (13 hectares)**

1

A good beginners loch, absolutely crammed with fish in the four to six-ounce class and guaranteeing success with a team of small (12-14) flies of almost any pattern. The loch is shallow, and waders are useful as the best fishing is about thirty yards or more out. It fishes well at all times, in all places and in all conditions, though south and east shores are probably best.

LOWER LOCH HATRAVAT and UPPER LOCH HATRAVAT

Location: **Take peat road to the right of the A857 Stornoway to Ness road in Upper Barvas, just before the old church and big bend. Park near the main road as the peat road is unsuitable for most cars. Ten minutes walking will take you to the Lower loch and a further ten to fifteen to the Upper loch.**
Grid References: **376515 and 384511**
Areas: **25 and 10 acres (10 and 4 hectares)**

Good trout in both lochs, averaging six to eight ounces in Lower Loch and rather bigger in Upper Loch. Fish from well back to begin with as good trout lie close in. Peaty bottom requires care when wading. Both lochs fish best in a south breeze, especially in May-June and again in September. Expect a bag of two to four fish which fight (and eat) extremely well.

LOCH SMINIG

Location: **West of the A857 road between Upper Barvas and Ballantrushal. Turn left at the cattle grid in Upper Barvas on the A857 Stornoway to Ness road. The walk to the loch is about ten minutes.**
Grid Reference: **364528**
Area: **17 acres (7 hectares)**

This twin loch is shallow: wading and long casting are recommended. Trout around six to eight ounces are numerous and come readily to a team of small dark flies such as Black Pennell, Bibio, Mallard and Claret and Dark Olive.

Best months are April to June and September, especially in the evenings. Expect a bag of around four to six trout.

LOCHAN HATRAVAT

Location: Not to be confused with the west coast lochs of the same name already mentioned. This one is on the east side of Lewis. Take the A857 road to Ness, turning off to the right at Lionel on the B8015 road, then continuing on the peat road due south to the shielings at Cuishader where you can park. Follow the burn past Loch Bacavat Cross to the south-west then head due south. The whole walk will take you about forty-five minutes, but it is tough going!

Grid Reference: 533553

Area: 32 acres (13 hectares)

The loch is dammed and supplies water to the village of South Dell. The main body of the loch is dark and peaty, seeming to hold only small fish. However, the two arms at the south end hold good fish to over three pounds.

Though bait and spinner are much used, the loch responds to fly fishing with dark flies in sizes 12 and 10, especially in a south wind. Despite the loch's dour reputation a memorable capture is always possible.

LOCH TANA

Location: A very remote loch. Proceed as for Lochan Hatravat as far as parking at the Cuishader shielings. A two-hour walk over rough moor to the south-west will bring you to the loch. Take the usual precautions for walking the moor: carry a whistle, a map and a compass, and leave word where you are going. Sea fog (haar) is a regular occurrence in this area.

Grid Reference: 492546

Area: 10 acres (4 hectares)

Despite the effort required to get there the loch could well reward any angler willing to make the considerable trek: a recent bag of four trout weighed thirteen pounds! These were taken on spinner, but the loch is so rarely fished that fly also does well. For anyone wishing to fish for big brown trout in wild and beautiful terrain, this is the loch to try.

A stiff south wind is best, with May, June and September the good months.

LOCH MOR

Location:	**Ten minutes walk south of Loch Tana, this is another loch with a big reputation locally.**
Grid Reference:	**495543**
Area:	**25 acres (10 hectares)**

Much bigger than Loch Tana, it has a group of islands at the west end where large trout have been caught, mainly on bait and spinner. Like Tana, it can rarely have been fished with fly, and the fly-fisher making the considerable effort to reach Loch Tana should also fish Loch Mor, and a heavily-laden journey back to the car could be the result.

Flies in sizes 12 and 10 are recommended. Fish close in over the drop-off, especially in a stiffish south wind.

THE WEST SIDE

This section has a wide variety of lochs, from the early-fishing ones of the Atlantic seaboard to the hill and moor lochs of the interior. However, most of them are within easy to moderate walking distance.

In this section there are references to 'The Pentland Road'. This road runs westwards from the east end of Loch Vatandip at GR364338 to Breasclete and north-westwards from a junction at GR267363 to Carloway.

LOCH BACAVAT

Location: **Best approached by a steep westward climb from a point on the A857 Stornoway to Barvas road at the bridge over the Cliastul River (GR 388453). The Barvas River requires wading to gain its western side, but this presents no problem unless the river is in spate.**
Grid Reference: **365450**
Area: **17 acres (7 hectares)**

The loch is stony-bottomed and the south bank is more readily fishable, producing trout of about eight ounces.

LOCH AORAIDH

Location: **Lies about half a mile north of Loch Bacavat.**
Grid Reference: **360455**
Area: **20 acres (8 hectares)**

More difficult wading than Loch Bacavat because it is more stony, but it contains many trout, though rather smaller in size.

The walk up to these two lochs can be rewarded by sightings of deer amongst the peat hags and duck on the lochs.

LOCH URRAHAG

Location: **On the A858, 2 miles from the road junction at Barvas.**
Grid Reference: **325480**
Area: **193 acres (78 hectares)**

This loch is one and a quarter miles long and the end is at the roadside. There is easy access to various points by peat roads.

Fish of up to one pound used to be fairly plentiful on this loch but in recent years only the occasional one has been taken.

Six to ten ounces is now the normal size, but the loch would fish better from a boat as bigger fish can be seen rising in the evening, out of reach of the bank fisher.

It fishes best during May, June and September with September being the best month; though recently it has been a consistently good loch in any weather and at any time of the year, especially late in the day.

Loch Bruthadail at the southern tip of Loch Urrahag can be fished from late March onwards, and is good with flies during April and May and again in September. Trout are in the six to eight-ounce bracket but average size goes up to ten ounces late in season. The large bay at the south end and the bay in the north-west shore where a burn runs in are productive.

This is also a good beginners loch.

LOCH SPEALDRAVAT MOR

Location: **Close to and east of Loch Urrahag.**
Grid Reference: **328474**
Area: **30 acres (12 hectares)**

Easy access is by a peat road on the loch side. The loch fishes best during May, June and July when trout from eight to ten ounces are fairly plentiful. After April there is a bloom on the water which does not then fish well except with bait. Not an easy loch to wade.

Best parts are the west side, the bay at the southern end and mid-way on the east side.

LOCH BREIVAT

Location: **Due south of Loch Spealdravat Mor.**
Grid Reference: **330455**
Area: **217 acres (88 hectares)**

A very shallow loch but easily and safely waded, with good trout between eight ounces and a pound.

LOCH GRINAVAT

Location: **At the village of Bragar on the A858 road.**
Grid Reference: **295475**
Area: **15 acres (6 hectares)**

2

An early loch which becomes weedy after June. The west side and south-west corner, both of which can be waded, are best. The trout run from eight ounces to a pound.

Loch an Duna (Duin) is half a mile to the west of Grinavat. It is very stony and not easily waded. A likely bag would be six to eight trout averaging eight to ten ounces, but there are bigger ones about. The south shore is probably the best.

Loch Ordais is near the sea, north of Loch an Duna. The trout are big and few, but they are of very high quality. It is an early loch which becomes unfishable after June because of the weed growth. The west bank up to where the burn runs in can be good. The Ke-He, size 10, on bob or dropper, has done well here.

LOCH A' BHAILE

Location: **North of Shawbost beside the sea.**
Grid Reference: **255474**
Area: **62 acres (25 hectares)**

A very early loch which becomes impossibly weedy after June. The large bay on the south side is good. Trout average eight ounces but there are some around the pound mark.

LOCH RAOINAVAT

Location: **Half a mile west of South Shawbost, adjacent to the A853 road.**
Grid Reference: **235460**
Area: **74 acres (30 hectares)**

Trout run to over a pound, especially round the small islands. A portable boat would be useful.

LOCH LANGAVAT

Location: **To the left of the branch road to the village of Dalmore.**
Grid Reference: **215440**
Area: **25 acres (10 hectares)**

The loch can be approached from the branch road to Dalmore or from a point a quarter of a mile on the Carloway side of its junction with the A858.

The loch has the reputation of being very dour but for the angler who perseveres and does not object to using bait or spinner it can prove very good on some days.

The trout are big and some up to four pounds have been taken but the big ones seldom rise to the fly. Flies if used should be fished very deeply — size 10 normally but size 8 on a windy day.

A good fishing point is the peninsula at the south-east end of the loch.

LOCH FASGRO

Location: **Near the village of Carloway.**
Grid Reference: **205415**
Area: **25 acres (10 hectares)**

This is the reservoir for the Carloway water supply and since the loch was dammed and the water level raised the trout have shown much improvement in size and quality, though whether this improvement is continuing is doubtful.

Since the raising of the water level the loch has become dangerous for wading and care should be taken by anyone attempting to do so. The trout vary in size from six ounces to three-quarters of a pound.

LOCH BORASDALE

Location: **Near the Carloway end of the Pentland Road.**
Grid Reference: **212408**
Area: **25 acres (10 hectares)**

The trout in this loch vary from six to twelve ounces. It is usually best in the evenings during May and June when fly proves very successful. It would be well worth taking a portable boat to this loch in order to fish it properly.

Between Loch Borasdale and the A858 road there are two triangle-shaped lochs — **Loch Cliasam Creag** and **Loch Bealach na Sgail** (the latter is not named on the Ordnance Survey map). These are more easily approached from the main road, anywhere in the vicinity of the Doune Braes Hotel. Approaching the loch from the Pentland Road is a much longer route. However if you are fishing Loch Borasdale, then Loch Cliasam Creag is about a fifteen-minute walk away.

2

The trout on both of these lochs vary from six to ten ounces.

LOCH AN DUIN

Location: **At the village of Doune Carloway (Dun Carloway).**
Grid Reference: **188408**
Area: **25 acres (10 hectares)**

The trout average ten ounces and some up to one and a half pounds have been taken on bait. April and May are the best months with September also quite good. During these months the loch is good with fly in the late evening but worm proves more successful during the daytime.

The loch takes its name from the stone tower or broch, one of the 500 around the north and west of Scotland, which date from the first three centuries of our era and whose builders and purpose remain mysterious.

LOCH ALMAISTEAN

Location: **Two miles south of Carloway, lying west of the Pentland Road.**
Grid Reference: **218395**
Area: **25 acres (10 hectares)**

This loch and **Loch Fionnacleit (Iunacleit)** beside it, situated in a very hilly part of the moor, are very good for fly fishing during both May and June. Trout are mostly about half a pound with the occasional three-quarter pounder. The easiest access is from the Pentland Road.

LOCH A' BHAILE

Location: **At Tolsta Chaolais near the road.**
Grid Reference: **197385**
Area: **37 acres (15 hectares)**

This loch fishes best during April, May and June. From July onwards weeds emerge and some parts are not easily fished. A portable boat would be useful. The trout average half a pound and are of good quality.

The loch is at sea level and with a high tide the sea enters it. During that time some seatrout may be taken.

LOCH NA MUILNE

Location: **Approaching from Garynahine, to the left of the main road just beyond the junction of the A858 and the branch road to Tolsta Chaolais.**
Grid Reference: **205378**
Area: **25 acres (10 hectares)**

Reseeding on some of the adjacent land has been beneficial to the fauna on the bottom of this loch, resulting in more food being available for the trout, which have increased noticeably in size. The average is half a pound and in a recent year a few up to one pound were taken on bait. The late evening is best for fly fishing.

LOCH EILASTER (EILEASTAIR)

Location: **Between Loch Laxavat Iorach and the A858 road.**
Grid Reference: **220380**
Area: **27 acres (11 hectares)**

Another loch situated in very hilly country. There is no easy walk to this one and unless one is fishing some of the other lochs in the Pentland Road area the best starting point is from the A858 in the vicinity of Loch na Muilne.

The trout are similar to those on Loch Almaistean and are very good with fly during May, June and September.

LOCH LAXAVAT (LACAVAT) IORACH, LOCH LAXAVAT ARD, and CARLOWAY RIVER

These waters are controlled by the **Carloway Angling Association** from whom permission to fish should be obtained. Try the Carloway Post Office.

LOCH AIRIGH SEIBH

Location:	**To the north side of the Pentland Road, opposite Loch Laxavat Ard.**
Grid Reference:	**260386**
Area:	**57 acres (23 hectares)**

Though less than half a mile from the road this is not an easy part of the moor to walk. The trout average half a pound and the loch fishes best in June and September.

There is the possibility of salmon or seatrout at the end of the season or as early as July if there has been a heavy spate.

Successive half miles south-eastwards are **Loch Mor a' Ghrianain** and **Loch nan Cleitichean** which are good early lochs.

LOCH BHARAVAT

Location: **On the A858 road near the village of Callanish.**
Grid Reference: **224342**
Area: **17 acres (7 hectares)**

There are two approaches to this loch. One is by a ten-minute walk over the hill from the church at Callanish. The other is by taking the branch road to the right a mile north of the church, which takes you to within a few minutes of the north end of the loch.

Though it is sometimes said that the trout here are in good condition from mid-March onwards this is not strictly correct. Some are in reasonable condition by then but April and May are the best months. After this they do not take well.

They vary from six to ten ounces and are good strong sporting fish. A Blue Zulu is particularly good in late March.

The far side of the loch is best, as well as the island at the southern end which is accessible with waders and at times with wellingtons. Though the bottom here is peaty it is reasonably firm and quite safe to cross.

LOCH AN TUIM

Location: **Near the junction of the Pentland Road and Breasclete branch road.**
Grid Reference: **255358**
Area: **54 acres (22 hectares)**

It is not easy to fly fish this loch from the bank. The bottom is stony and the wading difficult but with a favourable wind parts can be fished. It is better however from a boat and it is worth taking a portable one as the loch is close to the road. Bait fishing from the bank has proved more successful than fly. The trout vary from six to ten ounces.

From Loch an Tuim towards Breasclete there is a string of lochs on the left hand side of the road all of which contain hundreds of very small trout.

One loch in particular is very good for children or beginners learning to cast a fly. It is practically impossible not to hook a fish on this loch with a cast of dark flies, size 12. It is a small loch with an end to the road and a peat road running down the right hand bank. Although not named on the map it is easily recognised.

On the right hand side of the road and equidistant between the Pentland Road and Breasclete is **Loch an Fhraoich**. This loch fishes best in April with fly or bait but is not so good during the rest of the season. The trout are mostly under the half pound.

LOCH NAM BREAC

Location:	**About three-quarters of a mile north of the Pentland Road and best reached by ascending the stream Fionn Allt Beag.**
Grid Reference:	**282370**
Area:	**54 acres (22 hectares)**

A good early loch and easily fished, though the western bank is rather broken up by small ravines through the peat. Numerous small trout around six ounces.

2

A little to the north is **Loch Airigh Mhic Fhionnlaidh Duibh** which is rather reedy and muddy but which is a good beginners loch. Close to the west side of this loch, but over a watershed, lies the larger **Loch nan Caorach** (GR 275380). The north side is stony-bottomed but fishes easily, yielding trout up to eight ounces.

LOCH CEANN ALLAVAT

Location:	**About half a mile to the north of Loch nan Caorach and just under two miles from the Pentland Road.**
Grid Reference:	**277390**
Area:	**35 acres (14 hectares)**

This is an attractive loch with its several small rhododendron-clad islets, bays and jutting points. From the side one is fishing into good deep water in several places.

Trout are usually between eight and twelve ounces but some very good ones of over two pounds have been taken. Late in the season, especially after a spate, seatrout appear in this loch and in the two downstream.

The remains of several roofless shielings will give the wandering angler some shelter in bad weather.

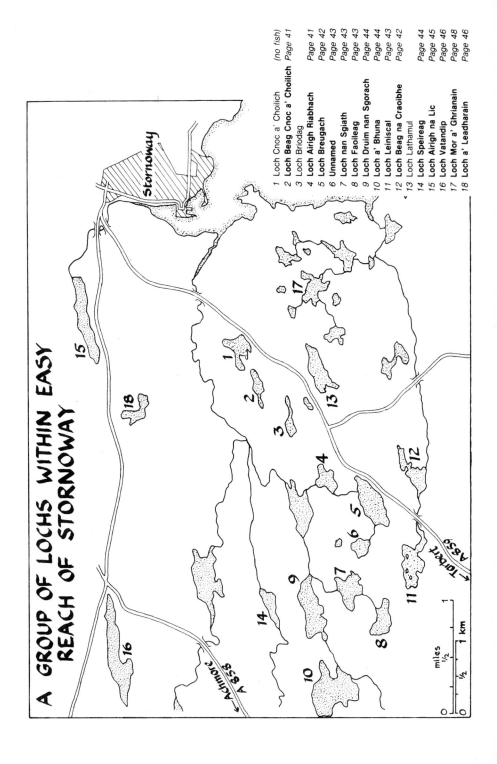

A GROUP OF LOCHS WITHIN EASY REACH OF STORNOWAY

1 Loch Cnoc a' Choilich   (no fish)
2 **Loch Beag Cnoc a' Choilich** Page 41
3 Loch Briodag
4 **Loch Airigh Riabhach**   Page 41
5 **Loch Breugach**   Page 42
6 Unnamed   Page 43
7 **Loch nan Sgiath**   Page 43
8 **Loch Faoileag**   Page 43
9 **Loch Druim nan Sgorach**   Page 44
10 **Loch a' Bhuna**   Page 44
11 **Loch Leiniscal**   Page 43
12 **Loch Beag na Craoibhe**   Page 42
13 Loch Lathamul
14 **Loch Speireag**   Page 44
15 **Loch Airigh na Lic**   Page 45
16 **Loch Vatandip**   Page 46
17 **Loch Mor a' Ghrianain**   Page 48
18 **Loch a' Leadharain**   Page 46

Stornoway

Achmore A 858

Tarbert A859

miles
½   1
0   ½   1 km

THE EAST SIDE

The southern and western borders of this area, arbitrarily drawn because of the absence of a clear geographical boundary, merge with part of section 5 (West and Centre). Stornoway has been taken as the starting off point to a large number of lochs of all descriptions, incorporating some in the aptly named district of North Lochs.

A GROUP OF LOCHS WITHIN EASY REACH OF STORNOWAY

The first loch we come to on the A859 main road from Stornoway to Tarbert is Loch Cnoc a' Choilich and is mentioned only because it should be avoided as it holds no trout — at least if it does no one sees them!

LOCH BEAG CNOC A' CHOILICH

Location:	**Adjacent to the loch mentioned above and ten minutes walk from the road.**
Grid Reference:	**390316**
Area:	**17 acres (7 hectares)**

The trout on this loch average half a pound and are of very good quality. The occasional three-quarter pounder has been taken at the rocks on the north side which is the most productive part. The fish do not usually rise well to fly except in May and early June.

LOCH AIRIGH RIABHACH

Location:	**First loch to the west of the A859 south of its junction with the B897 (Grimshader).**
Grid Reference:	**377307**
Area:	**27 acres (11 hectares)**

Trout are in good condition from May onwards with an average weight of ten ounces, with some larger fish about, but this can be a difficult loch. The south-east corner and the whole of the south and east sides are best.

The trout on **Loch Uisg' an t-Soluis** a short distance north-west from Loch Airigh Riabhach are mostly under half a pound, but from July onwards some seatrout and the odd salmon are distinct possibilities.

LOCH BREUGACH

Location: **Adjacent to the main road half a mile south of the junction of the A859 and B897.**
Grid Reference: **375300**
Area: **44 acres (18 hectares)**

This loch has two boats which can be hired from the Stornoway Angling Association through Sportsworld, Stornoway.

From the bank fly-fishing is difficult, but bait and spinner work well as fish tend to lie well out. Boat fishing with fly can be very good with the average weight around ten ounces, though fish of over two pounds have been taken and one of around five pounds lost! The loch fishes best in the late evening with a good south-westerly breeze, but the dedicated boat-fisher can be successful in almost any conditions using dark flies along with Claret Bumble, Invicta, Blue Zulu, etc.

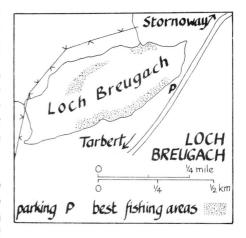

For the bank fisher the best parts are the side nearest the road, and on the far side around the outlet of the stream to Loch Airigh Riabhach. Try to keep well clear of nesting terns on the islets half-way along the north shore.

When casting be careful of the overhead high-voltage lines on two sides of the loch.

LOCH BEAG NA CRAOIBHE

Location: **A short distance south of Loch Breugach on the opposite side of the A859.**
Grid Reference: **376294**
Area: **25 acres (10 hectares)**

The trout on this loch are plentiful and, though small, are of good quality. The bigger ones move inshore in the evenings and rise well to the fly. Best parts are along the road side and the whole eastern section of the loch. This is a good loch for beginners of any age.

42

LOCH LEINISCAL

Location: **Close to the A859, opposite Loch Beag na Craoibhe.**
Grid Reference: **365295**
Area: **35 acres (14 hectares)**

The trout are bigger than on Loch Beag na Craoibhe and are best on the side of the loch furthest from the road. The island, which is normally accessible (in wellingtons), is also a good spot. A good breeze is necessary. Beware of overhead high-voltage lines.

LOCH NAN SGIATH

Location: **Half a mile west of Loch Breugach.**
Grid Reference: **362303**
Area: **27 acres (11 hectares)**

The trout are of good quality and average three-quarters of a pound. Some up to one and a half pounds have been taken. They do not usually rise to fly though the odd one is caught with fly fished near the bottom. Most of the bigger fish have been taken on bait. But the six-ounce size rise well to the fly, and the fly-fisher may be well advised to keep trying for something larger. Usually dour.

Between Loch nan Sgiath and Loch Breugach there is a small loch which is not named on the map **(GR 366300)**. The trout here are one and a half to over two pounds but only worm has any success. Very dour.

A short distance to the north there is yet another very small **unnamed loch** (GR 370305) which in mid-season is overgrown with weeds and looks as if it could not possibly hold any fish but trout over two pounds have been taken there, and as on the previous loch worm seems to be the only lure to entice them.

LOCH FAOILEAG

Location: **A short distance to the south-west of Loch nan Sgiath.**
Grid Reference: **358298.**
Area: **27 acres (11 hectares)**

Another loch with good quality trout averaging three-quarters of a pound. Best on the north side near the rocky corner by the stream connecting it to Loch nan Sgiath. Similarly the south side opposite this point. Though the bottom is not particularly good for it, wading is usually necessary here, especially if fly fishing, in order to reach out to where the trout are lying.

LOCH A' BHUNA

Location:	**On the A858 about six miles from Stornoway on the east side of the road.**
Grid Reference:	**346305**
Area:	**77 acres (31 hectares)**

Less than ten minutes walk from the road this loch was at one time stocked and has a good supply of good quality, very pink-fleshed trout, mostly under half a pound with the odd three-quarter pounder.

Anyone taking a portable boat to this loch who has no objection to fishing by trolling a cast of flies could get quite a basket. This method has in the past resulted in some very good catches for strangely enough the fish do not rise so readily to a cast fly.

A short distance further eastwards into the moor from Loch a' Bhuna are **Loch Druim nan Sgorach** and then northwards **Loch Speireag**. Though there are occasional reports of trout over one pound from both of these lochs the more usual size is six to eight ounces.

Just beyond Loch a' Bhuna and on the opposite side of the road we come to **Loch nan Eilean** where the trout are similar in size and quality and are very easily fished from the bank.

LOCH AIRIGH NA LIC

Location: **Two miles from Stornoway on the A858 (Stornoway — Achmore).**
Grid Reference: **400342**
Area: **49 acres (20 hectares)**

This roadside loch is not beautiful, with a quarry on one side, a rubbish tip just over the hill to the north, and litter along the shore, but it has its attractions. The trout average six ounces though bigger ones are occasionally taken.

However, after a heavy spate in July the first seatrout ascend the Glen River and can give good sport till the end of September, not only in the late evening to flies around 10 and 8 in size but also during the day to 10s, 12s or even 14s on light tackle, even in very low winds and bright sun. Waders are useful at the town end where wading to no further than below your knees allows you to cover the sunken weed beds beyond which the seatrout often lie. The north-west of the loch is another good place for seatrout. There is always the remote possibility of a salmon. Several have been seen, and one was caught a few years ago.

Standard loch patterns work well, especially Black Pennell, the Zulus and the Butchers. Try the very simply-dressed Donegal Blue on the bob (sizes 12 to 8).

Both sides of the loch are fishable, the north side being approached by taking the branch road through Maryhill, three hundred yards beyond the junction of the A858 and A859 roads.

LOCH AIRIGH NA LIC
best fishing areas
Bayhead River
¼ mile
¼   ½ km
Loch Airigh na Lic
←Achmore
Stornoway→

LOCH A' LEADHARAIN (LEADARAIN)

Location:	**Half a mile west of Loch Airigh na Lic and to the south of the A858.**
Grid Reference:	**386335**
Area:	**17 acres (7 hectares)**

This loch is not within sight of the road but a walk of ten or fewer minutes will take you there. The trout average three-quarters of a pound and the loch fishes from May onwards. Some are taken on fly in the evening but bait is more successful. Unfortunately eels are plentiful and can be a nuisance to the baitfisher at times.

LOCH VATANDIP

Location:	**Five miles from Stornoway, just west of the junction of the A858 and the B8010 (Pentland Road).**
Grid Reference:	**355336**
Area:	**57 acres (23 hectares)**

This loch has two boats owned by the Stornoway Angling Association which can be hired from Sportsworld, Stornoway.

It is an early and often difficult loch, April and May being the best months, but it can be fished during the whole season along both its sides.

The trout vary from six to twelve ounces, but much bigger ones are taken on fly, bait and spinner especially in April and May. Some seatrout enter the loch late in the season.

Care should be taken to return any smolts unharmed.

LOCH MOR A' CHOCAIR

Location:	**Near Loch Vatandip on the north side of the B8010.**
Grid Reference:	**348345**
Area:	**27 acres (11 hectares)**

Good with fly in the late evening. The trout are mostly under half a pound and are of good quality. The north side is probably the best part and again care should be taken with smolts.

Loch Beag a' Chocair, just to the west of Loch Mor a' Chocair, is a small loch with small trout in it, but late in the season it often has a run of seatrout and salmon.

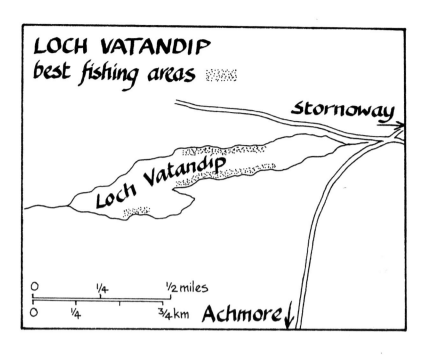

LOCH VATANDIP
best fishing areas

Stornoway

Loch Vatandip

0   1/4   1/2 miles

0   1/4   3/4 km   Achmore

THE ARNISH LOCHS

This is a group of early lochs, but they can be fished throughout the season especially in the evenings. They can also be good late in the season.

LOCH AIRIGH NAN GLEANN

Location: **Best approached by a short peat road leading off the A859 Stornoway to Tarbert road near the east end of Loch Lathamul (GR 393308), the latter being picturesque but containing no trout!**

Grid Reference: **398305**

Area: **12 acres (5 hectares)**

The loch has some steep banks with deep water on its south side and a shallow, muddy bottom off the marshy, reseeded west shore.

Some good trout up to two pounds are taken each year almost entirely by spinning or bait fishing. When fish do come to the fly they are around twelve ounces. Blue Zulu, Grouse and Claret, Grouse and Green recommended.

47

LOCH MOR A' GHRIANAIN

Location:	**Best approached by the same route as for Loch Airigh nan Gleann.**
Grid Reference:	**404308**
Area:	**12 acres (5 hectares)**

A fairly deep loch with steep banks in places. In recent years it has not fished well in early season but it improves in August and September with mainly pink-fleshed trout of between eight and ten ounces.

LOCH BEAG A' GHRIANAIN

Location:	**Due south of Loch Mor a' Ghrianain.**
Grid Reference:	**402305**
Area:	**10 acres (4 hectares)**

This loch is not named on the map, and is about ten minutes walk from the previous loch. Good quality small trout are plentiful and rise well to the fly.

LOCH AIRIGH AN SGAIRBH

Location:	**On the Arnish moor, just north-east from Loch Mor a' Ghrianain.**
Grid Reference:	**408310**
Area:	**20 acres (8 hectares)**

Known locally as the Piper Loch. The loch, with the average trout being ten ounces, fishes best early in the season, late March and April being the best months.

The best fishing areas are by the small island on the west side, near the green knoll at the southern end and at the rocky point on the east.

LOCH MOR A' CHROTAICH

Location: **On the Arnish moor, south of the 'Piper Loch'.**
Grid Reference: **411303**
Area: **27 acres (11 hectares)**

Another loch with a local name — 'The Frying Pan'. Like the previous loch this one also fishes best early in the season and trout are similar in size and quality.

The best part is the north shore near the stream from Loch Mor a' Ghrianain. Between the narrow section and the small bay on the east side is also a favourite spot.

There is another small loch at the southern end of Loch Airigh an Sgairbh from which trout up to one and a half pounds have been taken but bait seems the only way to catch them, and not very often at that!

Access to the last three lochs can be from the A859 road or the Arnish road or, if anyone wishes to walk the whole way from Stornoway, through the Castle Grounds and on for a mile or so beyond the foot-bridge at the Creed River. If approaching from the A859 keep between Loch Mor a' Ghrianain and the small loch to the north of it. There are two fences to cross but it is an easy and pleasant walk.

3

UNNAMED LOCH

Location: **Ten minutes walk to the south-east of Loch Airigh nan Gleann.**
Grid Reference: **400300**
Area: **10 acres (4 hectares)**

This small kidney-shaped loch becomes very weedy in high summer, but it is remarkable for a plentiful supply of very golden-bellied trout, mainly of six ounces and under, which rise well to the fly and fight with vigour.

LOCHS FARTHER OUT FROM STORNOWAY

LOCH MOR AN STAIRR (STARR)

Location: **Five miles from Stornoway on the A857 Stornoway-Barvas road.**
Grid Reference: **395385**
Area: **72 acres (29 hectares)**

This is the main reservoir for the Stornoway water supply. Trout range from half a pound to one and a half pounds with perhaps three-quarters of a pound average. Fish can be taken very close to the bank in the evening, especially on the south side where an abundance of flies is blown from the heather into the loch.

The nearest point on the road is at Loch Roisnavat, but from there it is not an easy stretch of moor to walk. The easier though much longer route is from the waterworks whence you can follow a rough track.

LOCH ORASAY

Location: **One and a half miles along the B897 (Grimshader) from its junction with the A859.**
Grid Reference: **390280**
Area: **121 acres (49 hectares)**

This loch with easy access from the Grimshader road has numerous small islands and one larger one about half a mile long in the middle leaving a narrow channel at the south end, and another with numerous bays at the north.

The trout vary in size, from half a pound upwards with perhaps three-quarters of a pound average. Quite a few up to two pounds are taken during the season and the odd three pounder, all of very good quality.

Fish can be taken in various conditions of weather and it is difficult to say which is the best for this loch. Good catches have been taken in a howling north-west wind with heavy rain as well as with a stiff south-east breeze and bright sunshine. In what would seem to be the perfect conditions you might draw a blank. A very temperamental loch indeed, but it holds good trout.

Charr of up to three quarters of a pound or one pound are taken frequently but only on worm or at odd times with a spinner.

The best fishing areas are the bays and narrows at the north end, both sides of the peninsula at the Grimshader road side of the loch, the east and west sides of the narrows at the southern end and at the south-west side opposite the small island.

The loch has become more difficult in the last few years after the level was raised in a water-supply scheme. Time will tell whether it will recover its former quality as a fishing loch.

Loch Innseag to the east of Loch Orasay and a short distance over the road fishes well in June and again late in the season. Average tends to be small, but eight to ten-ounce trout can come readily to the fly, especially around the wooded islands in the southern half.

Most of the other lochs in the vicinity of Loch Orasay have gone back in recent years and for the time being are not worth mentioning. It is to be hoped that they may recover in time, however.

LOCH TOM AN FHEIDH

3

Location:	**East of Loch Innseag about 30 minutes walk from the road.**
Grid Reference:	**412285**
Area:	**30 acres (12 hectares)**

This is an early loch and fishes best from late March to the end of May. The trout vary in size but average eight ounces. Tapeworm have sometimes been found recently in trout from this loch. Check carefully, especially any fish that comes in too easily for its size.

The Cardinal, not a fashionable fly these days, has a local reputation for taking the bigger trout from the lochs in this area. Grouse and Claret is always reliable.

Some from three-quarters to two pounds are taken early in the season but the loch is not very productive after June.

The best parts are near the narrows and in the bay at the south-east end where the bigger ones lie.

LOCH ARD AIRIGH A' GHILLE RUAIDH

Location: **Access from a small quarry on the south-east side of the A859 Stornoway to Tarbert road, about half a mile from the little stream which joins Lochs Leiniscal and Beag na Craoibhe. This is a good starting point for fishing several lochs on this part of the moor. A ten-minute walk to the south leads to the circular-shaped loch lying in a bowl of moorland.**

Grid Reference: **372283**

Area: **5 acres (2 hectares)**

Apart from a weedy area along the south shore, the rest of the loch can be fished into a good depth of water from the banks, and good, fighting trout up to 12 ounces, though mainly in the six- to eight-ounce range, rise well to the fly.

Immediately to the east is a separate **small loch** where golden-tinged trout of up to six or eight ounces also rise well to the fly.

Other lochs in the area, Loch Airigh an t-Sagairt, Loch nan Laogh and Loch Beinn na Gainmheich (Gainmhich), are less profitable. Try to avoid disturbing the area around Loch Airigh an t-Sagairt in early summer (May-June) as it is a nesting site for gulls and greylag geese.

LOCH URAVAL

Location: **The south-easternmost of a group of named lochs all lying north of the TV mast on Eitshal (223 metres) near Achmore, but best approached from a point (GR 300350) on the Pentland Road.**

Grid Reference: **305327**

Area: **69 acres (28 hectares)**

This loch shallows gradually on its north-west shore but is fairly easily waded. The southern shore is steeper and the water deeper. Trout varying in size between six to ten ounces can be taken throughout the season: though the loch has a reputation for being an early one it probably fishes best in May and June. The rocky point on the south shore and the shallow area around the island are recommended.

The trout in **Loch nan Cnamh** are slightly bigger, those in **Loch Airigh nan Sloc** are difficult, and the northern part of **Loch na Moine** has many naturally rising small trout.

LOCH NAN GEADH

Location:	North of the Pentland Road, this is best approached from GR 300350, being reached after a steady climb of about twenty minutes.
Grid reference:	305363
Area:	20 acres (8 hectares)

A small loch, just under half a mile in length. Its outlet at the east end has silted up, making the south-east and south sides marshy. Take care after a wet spell.

The fish are of good size and quality, but the loch can be very dour. Good flies are Teal and Green and Blue Zulu. The west and north-west sides fish best.

LOCH THOTA (TOBHTA) BRIDEIN

Location:	Beside the road linking Cameron Terrace with Achmore.
Grid Reference:	335275
Area:	67 acres (27 hectares)

3

This loch used to be full of small trout but after the reseeding on the west bank the size and quality of the trout have increased considerably. This is a good early loch which also fishes well in the evenings later in the season.

A west or south-west wind allows the fly-fisher to cover the whole west shore. Wading is fairly easy, but most trout tend to lie close in, especially in the spring. The south end has so far produced the biggest trout, up to a pound in some cases. This is also a good area if you have a portable boat as there is a productive weed bed some distance off shore.

Very good bags have been taken on size 12 and 10 flies including Invicta, Kate McLaren, Soldier Palmer, Dunkeld, Haul a Gwynt and the Leven Spider, the last fished on the tail in sizes 14 to 16. In a good breeze, be prepared to raise the fly size to 8, when the Haul a Gwynt, usually best in small sizes, can be surprisingly effective. Be prepared, however, for the odd complete blank!

The road side can also produce nice trout, especially near the old fish cages, but the wind seldom favours the fly fisher. In such a case, try fishing a single large fly, such as the Ombudsman, on a short leader, casting across the wind, as the fish tend to lie among the breaking waves close in.

Park at the north end of the loch where there is a convenient spot.

LOCH ACHMORE

Location: **Below the crofts at the village of Achmore on the A858 road.**
Grid Reference: **310285**
Area: **106 acres (43 hectares)**

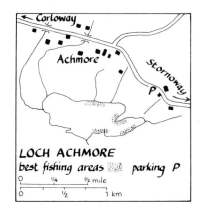

The good-quality trout average three-quarters of a pound. The loch fishes best during April, May, June and September. Not so productive during July and August but trout can still be taken. Best parts are the east side of the peninsula nearest the crofts, the south-east end of the loch and the rocky shore on the south side.

LOCH NAN RAMH

Location: **Beside the A858 road from Stornoway, about a mile from the village of Achmore.**
Grid reference: **327300**
Area: **12 acres (5 hectares)**

This roadside loch looks unpromising. It is generally shallow and wading is difficult along the road shore because of deep, muddy patches and boulders. The other shores are similarly boulder-strewn.

Yet the loch has a population of high-quality, pink-fleshed trout from six ounces to one and a half pounds, though often difficult to catch, and a reputed small run of seatrout in a wet end-of-season.

Bait fishers tend to fish the road shore and the small peninsula at the south-west corner. Fly fishing is best from the fence (and stile) at the north end round the loch clockwise to the peninsula already mentioned. Smallish flies are best, and a Blue Zulu on the bob fished from the peninsula in a good breeze in the evening can bring up big fish. A corixa imitation can work well as trout are often crammed with the natural.

The most convenient winds for fly-fishing are those from the north, east and south-east! This loch is an acquired taste and often proves difficult, but it can repay attention, especially late in the evening.

LOCH FOID

Location: **Due south of Loch Achmore.**
Grid Reference: **311279**
Area: **32 acres (13 hectares)**

Similar quality trout to Loch Achmore though perhaps smaller in size.

The loch is very good in September near the stream at the east end and also at the narrow section of the loch.

Good for fly fishing — there are no high banks to hinder casting. It is unnecessary but most of the loch can be waded.

The occasional salmon and seatrout may appear in the loch after heavy rain from late August onwards.

LOCH NA CRAOIBHE

Location: **Within easy reach of the two previous lochs.**
Grid Reference: **300277**
Area: **32 acres (13 hectares)**

The trout on the west side of the loch are generally smaller. The east side is best especially near the narrow neck between the loch itself and Loch nam Falcag. The average weight is ten ounces and many over one pound are taken.

If conditions are right fly can be very successful, particularly in the evening.

The trout on **Loch nam Falcag** which is connected to Loch na Craoibhe are not quite so good in size or quality but should not be ignored.

To the west of Loch nam Falcag there is a small rectangular and **unnamed loch** (GR287268) lying north and south. Because of the nature of the surrounding terrain it can easily be missed. Cross through the opening between Loch Iosal a' Bhruic and Loch nam Falcag walking uphill south-west and keeping a sharp look out to the right. Very good quality golden coloured trout averaging half a pound are fairly plentiful and they rise well to the fly.

The trout on **Loch Iosal a' Bhruic** are very plentiful but of poor quality and should be avoided except perhaps by beginners or children anxious to catch fish.

LOCH NA GAINHMICH

Location: **South of the village of Lochganvich, to the west of Achmore.**
Grid Reference: **285295**
Area: **101 acres (41 hectares)**

Can be fished round the whole perimeter, but the north-west shore is a favourite area. The trout are of good quality, averaging half a pound, and sometimes an occasional bigger one up to one pound is taken with bait at the small peninsula in the north-west corner. The fish tend to lie well out, and long casting is often necessary.

South and south-west from Loch na Gainmhich are **Loch na Creige Guirme, Loch Tana** and **Loch an Daimh**, all holding trout from six to eight ounces. A spinning lure can prove effective on Loch an Daimh when neither fly nor bait will work and some fish up to three-quarters of a pound have been taken in this way.

LOCH AN FHADA BHIG

Location: **Walking to this loch can be part of a very pleasant day's outing. The best approach is from GR 273305 on the A858 road skirting past the east side of the conifer plantation until one approaches the west side of Lochavat (GR 270286), a nice clean loch which fishes well early in the season and has good-quality trout up to twelve ounces. Then go on south to Loch Skapraid (Scapraid) (GR 268276), where one can still see the remains of the village of Scapraid, and catch trout averaging eight ounces. Go uphill from here to the west-south-west to Loch Gobhlaich (Gobhlach) (GR 256273) where there are bright and silvery trout of six to eight ounces. Loch an Fhada Bhig is a short walk to the south.**
Grid Reference: **252266**
Area: **22 acres (9 hectares)**

The water of this loch is unusually clear and it is a very pleasant one to fish. Although the east shore rises steeply, making it awkward for the fly-fisher's back-cast, fishing the fly along the shore can be very successful, and very good catches can be made near a little island (not shown on the map) half-way down the east bank. This shore shelves steeply, and trout lie close in to the water's edge. They are usually betwen ten and twelve ounces, sometimes bigger, and of excellent quality.

Ten minutes walk to the east lies **Loch an Eilean Chubhraidh** (GR 258266), unnamed on the map, which holds good quality trout of between six and ten ounces. The walk back to the A858 starting point will take you about an hour.

LOCH KEOSE

Location: See sketch map overleaf.
Grid Reference: 367225
Area: 89 acres (36 hectares)

This loch is privately owned and is open to guests at Handa, 18 Keose Glebe, Tel 0851 83334 (Mr and Mrs M Morrison). Boats are also available for hire to non-residents at the Tourist Board office and at Sportsworld, Stornoway. There are excellent jetty facilities. There is no charge for bank fishing.

There is a large natural population of trout up to eight ounces, not always well conditioned but the pink-fleshed ones make delicious eating and fight well above their weight. It is a good loch for the beginner, especially fishing from a boat.

The loch is one of the most beautiful in Lewis. Visitors may land on the island near the north end of the loch, which is an ideal spot for picnicking.

3

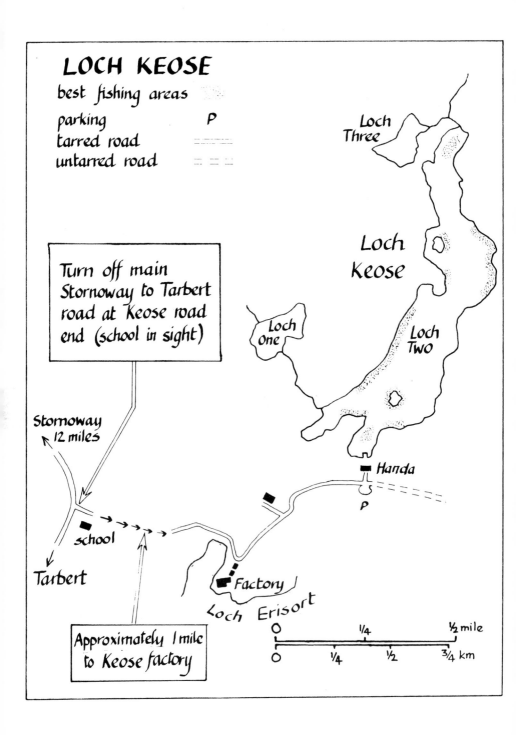

GREAT BERNERA

This beautiful island, reached by bridge, has good lochs all within easy reach of one another and easily accessible from the roads. The sea is never far away, and the Machiavellian angler can easily disappear from the family picnic on the lovely beaches for an hour's surreptitious fishing without being greatly missed.

LOCH GEAL

Location:	**By the roadside near the school at Breaclete.**
Grid Reference:	**159364**
Area:	**15 acres (6 hectares)**

Not named on OS maps and better known as the school loch this should not be confused with the Loch Geal *which is named on maps* by the roadside two miles further on.

Ground fertilisation on adjacent land has made an improvement in the size of the trout which are mostly between eight and twelve ounces, but fish of over two pounds, with the occasional three pounder, are taken every season. This loch probably contains the biggest trout in Bernera. The west side, furthest from the road, is best, especially for spinning, though weed growth can make spinning difficult after June. The trout also rise well to flies.

4

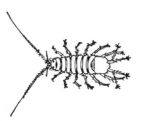

LOCH IONAIL

Location:	**A five-minute walk to the west of Loch Geal but more directly approached from the road between Breaclete and Hacklete.**
Grid Reference:	**156363**
Area:	**7 acres (3 hectares)**

This loch has a very good head of trout averaging eight ounces which usually rise well.

LOCH NA CEANNAMHOIR

Location: **To the south of Loch Geal but best approached from the main road to Breaclete.**
Grid Reference: **159356**
Area: **10 acres (4 hectares)**

Similar to Loch Ionail but with bigger trout averaging twelve ounces. Both lochs can be very good.

LOCH BARAVAT

Location: **Off the Breaclete-Hacklete road three-quarters of a mile beyond junction at Breaclete School.**
Grid Reference: **155355**
Area: **69 acres (28 hectares)**

There is room to park a car just short of the stream running from the north end of the loch to the sea. Go through the gate in the fence, over the hill, and the first bay you come to is one of the best parts to fish. The whole of the west side is good, free of obstructions, easily waded and very suitable for spinning.

The area for half a mile in both directions from the Dun on the east side is also good, and probably best around the inverted T bay and the fank to the south. The south end of the loch near Hacklete is also worth fishing.

This loch can be easily the best (and easily the stiffest) in Bernera. The trout are of excellent quality with an average weight of around the pound, and much bigger fish are there for the taking.

LOCH BREACLETE

Location: **Locally called Loch Mor, it lies immediately to the south and east of the village of Breaclete.**
Grid Reference: **164365**
Area: **40 acres (16 hectares)**

This is a very good loch for fly-fishing, especially in May/June, with trout averaging twelve to fourteen ounces. The west shore is best, and round the small island. Please avoid disturbing the terns which nest in the heather on the island.

LOCH NAN GEADRAISEAN and LOCH NA MUILNE

Location: **To the east of Loch Breaclete.**
Grid Reference: **168365**
Area: **15 acres (6 hectares)**

A causeway across the narrows divides this water into two separate lochs. The northern section is known as Loch na Muilne, but is not named on the OS map. This is best fished at the north-east shore where trout average half a pound. The southern section, Loch nan Geadraisean, is not recommended.

There is another **Loch na Muilne**, close by the roadside, in the north of the island at GR 148397 near Bosta. This can be an excellent loch, well worth fishing. The trout, though sometimes smallish, are white-fleshed but very sweet.

4

KIRKIBOST LOCHS

Location: **Not far from the village of Kirkibost in the south-east end of the island.**

Grid Reference: **180356**

Area: **30 acres (12 hectares)**

There are three lochs here: the top one, **Loch Gobhlach**; the middle loch **unnamed** on the map and connected to the former; and the bottom loch, **Loch na Craoibhaig**.

The best approach is by following the road through Kirkibost until you come near the pier at the bay at the harbour known as Dubh Thob. This takes you much closer to the lochs and takes far less time than it would to cross the moor from near the south end of Loch Breaclete, which some anglers are inclined to do.

The bottom loch is the best as far as size is concerned and the excellent quality trout average three-quarters of a pound. They do not rise well to the fly except in good conditions with a warm southerly breeze in the evening. Most are taken with bait fished on the bottom. The south end and the south-west corner are the best parts and the odd trout up to two pounds can be expected here.

Weed emerges after the beginning of July and parts of the loch are not easily fished.

The trout on the middle loch are not as big — average half a pound. The best parts are the bay in the south-east corner and near the stream at the north-west. The south-west side of the loch is shallow and not suitable for spinning.

The average size on the top loch is similar, but fish are more plentiful. A red/silver Mepp Spoon proves successful here.

The best parts are on the east side: from the stream up to the narrows, and the north side of the bay.

These last two lochs can be fished during the whole season but are best in June.

THE WEST AND CENTRE

This contains some of the most remote parts of Lewis where the walking can be long but the angling rewards great. It is the home of a great variety of wildlife, from the deer on the hills to the golden eagle patrolling the lower slopes, and trout invariably take when you are admiring it all.

Such a large area requires division into sections so that the discerning angler can have time to savour all its attractions.

SOVAL ANGLING ASSOCIATION LOCHS

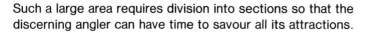

The following lochs on the Soval Estate are open to members of the **Soval Angling Association**: *Strandavat, an Sgath, Ibheir, Cuthaig, Airigh na Ceardaich, Roineval, an Tomain, na Croibhe, Dhomhnuill Bhig and Langavat* (fishing from the shore on the Soval section), as well as all lochs on the Soval Estate north of Loch Leurbost (a sea loch) and to the north of the road running from Achmore to the A859. Permits to fish these lochs are available from Association officials. Names, addresses and telephone numbers are in the current leaflet, 'Ag Iasgach — Fishing in the Western Isles', or may be had from the Western Isles Tourist Board.

Fishing on **LOCH LANGAVAT** on the Soval Estate is restricted to a maximum of four members of the Association on any one day. Non-members should apply personally to the Head Keeper, Mr John Macleod, Valtos Cottage, for permits (if available), proceeds from the sale of which go to local charities.

Four other estates — *Grimersta, Scaliscro, Morsgail and Aline* — border the loch and permission to fish should first be obtained from one of the proprietors concerned before setting out for this, the most beautiful loch in Lewis. The head waters of the famous Grimersta salmon fishings, Loch Langavat is the most extensive body of fresh water in Lewis, situated between the sea lochs Seaforth and Erisort on the east and Loch Resort and Little Loch Roag on the west.

5

The upper end of the loch lies among hills of over fifteen hundred feet and is a favourite haunt of the golden eagle, whilst the lower end borders on broad moorland.

There are three large, distinct basins, with numerous small islands and bays. The largest and deepest basin occupies the southern part of the loch, which is three and a quarter miles long and fully half a mile broad in the centre with a maximum depth of ninety-eight feet in a small area. The large basin is separated from the middle basin by a narrow channel where the depth is only nine feet.

The mid basin is the smallest of the three and is deepest at the south-western end, with a depth of ninety feet. It shallows towards the north-west.

The third section of the loch is similar in size to the first and contains many small islands but the shoreline is much more broken up. The largest area with a depth greater than twenty-five feet is at the south-west end — the depth is forty feet. The deepest part of this basin is near the lower end where the depth is sixty-five feet.

Taking a straight line from south-west to north-east, Langavat is seven and a quarter miles long but by taking the centre line of each basin the length increases to eight and a half miles.

The area is three and a half square miles, and the loch is the only loch in Lewis whose area exceeds one square mile. Nevertheless it is not the greatest loch in Lewis in terms of volume of water. That distinction belongs to Loch Suainaval in south-east Uig (whose area is about one quarter of that of Langavat) which has a maximum depth of two hundred and nineteen feet, a mean depth of one hundred and eight feet and which holds four hundred and fifty million cubic feet of water more than Loch Langavat.

There are various approaches to Loch Langavat, of which none is much under one hour's walk, but the walk is worth every minute even if only to view the grandeur of the scenery — on some days unsurpassable, especially from the hills above the upper basin. For best routes take local advice.

Brown trout are plentiful and in reasonable conditions one can expect a good catch. They vary in size from eight ounces to several pounds. Many in the two pound class are taken every season as well as the occassional one of six pounds and over. A weight of three-quarters of a pound is probably average and they rise well to the fly but the bigger ones are usually taken on bait or spinner.

Some parts of the loch are more productive than others, depending on whether one is fishing from boat or bank. As with most lochs a little local knowledge is of considerable importance and it would be advisable for the angler visiting the loch for the first time to make a few enquiries before setting off for a day's fishing. A little time spent on this will not be wasted.

In addition to the very good brown trout fishing many salmon and sea trout are taken during the season. Here again it is advisable to make some local enquiries.

Access to the main body of the Soval Angling Association lochs is best made by taking the peat road running off the A859 north from the police station in Balallan. Drive slowly and carefully, avoiding rocks and potholes, and park so as to allow free passage of other vehicles, tractors,. etc.

LOCH NA CROIBHE (CRAOIBHE)

Location: **In a hollow to the east of the peat road about three-quarters of a mile from the main A859.**
Grid Reference: **284218**
Area: **15 acres (6 hectares)**

The loch is stonier on its north-east, east and south sides, which fish better than its west side, which has a softer bottom. Reseeding schemes around the loch have further improved the very high quality fish, average weight eight ounces, with fish up to one pound, and occasionally two pounds, taken.

LOCH AIRIGH NA CEARDAICH and LOCH A' MHAIDE

Location: **These originally separate lochs, now one, appear on the map as Loch Airigh na Ceardaich. This name is now given to the loch to the east; the one to the west is known as Loch a' Mhaide, not Cuil Airigh na Flod as on the OS map. They lie north and north-west of Loch na Croibhe. Park at the end of the peat road where there is usually plenty of space.**
Grid References: **272223 and 277225**
Areas: **Roughly equal at 49 acres (20 hectares) each**

Loch a' Mhaide has two distinct types of trout: silver coloured fish up to eight ounces and larger, yellow-bellied ones with beautiful markings, sometimes reaching to over the pound.

Loch Airigh na Ceardaich trout are bigger on the average and the quality is excellent. The bay at the east end and the north shore can be very good.

Both lochs fish well to fly, bait and spinner but become difficult after June.

LOCH CUTHAIG

Location: **A short walk to the west of Loch na Croibhe.**
Grid Reference: **275215**
Area: **82 acres (33 hectares)**

This is a pleasant loch, often shallow and requiring wading, and sometimes temperamental, but it has beautiful trout! They average eight ounces, but fish of a pound and more are regularly taken. Most of the south shore and the east end are good, especially the rock at the north-east corner which, under normal conditions, can be reached wearing knee boots. The loch contains charr, but they seldom rise to the fly.

Fifty years ago when up to twenty cattle were walked daily along the shore on their way to graze at Druim Airigh Ruairidh their droppings fertilised the loch, making trout of two pounds common.

LOCH DHOMHNUILL (DHOMHNAILL) BHIG

Location: **A stiff fifteen-minute walk to the east of Loch na Croibhe but probably better approached either by walking up the west bank of Loch an Deasport at the east end of Balallan, or more directly by leaving the main A859 road at GR 299210.**
Grid Reference: **292220**
Area: **32 acres (13 hectares)**

There are two different trout types in this loch: the well-shaped silvery ones around six to eight ounces and the larger and darker ones around the pound. The wind tends to be funnelled from the north because of the shape of the surrounding hills, and the south end has heavy weed growth in late summer.

LOCH IBHEIR (IOMHAIR)

Location: **Half a mile to the north-west of Loch Cuthaig.**
Grid Reference: **265223**
Area: **27 acres (11 hectares)**

Good quality trout of up to eight ounces and larger ones of poor quality, dark brown in colour and unhealthy. The best fishing is on the east shore. Weed is a problem at the south end from June onwards.

On a good day this loch provides lively sport, but it can be very dour.

LOCH AN TOMAIN (TUAMACHAIN) and LOCH AN SGATH

Location: **Best approached by the peat road from the west end of Balallan at a point GR 272203 on the A859.**
Grid References: **258213 and 252212**
Areas: **27 acres (11 hectares) and 22 acres (9 hectares)**

Loch an Tomain is full of small trout which rise eagerly to the fly, and is thus an ideal loch for the learner fly-fisher — especially one with a cat.

Loch an Sgath has lots of good-quality silvery trout around five or six ounces which are lively fighters. Occasionally larger trout between eight to twelve ounces, differently coloured with large black spots and smaller red spots are taken. South and east shores are best.

Both lochs provide a pleasant rest for the angler moving more deeply into the moor seeking bigger fish.

THE LOCHS OF THE CENTRE

These are best approached by the same peat road from Balallan as for the Soval Angling Association Lochs, but be prepared for a good stiff walk of about one and a half hours.

If approaching the lochs to the west of Loch Fadagoa (Fadagoth) (GR 242240), such as Loch nan Eilean and Loch Roineval, it is essential to note that these lochs can be crossed at the following points: GR 242231, 238228, 234229. Approach to the lochs lying to the north of Loch Trealaval, and east of Loch Fadagoa, can only be made by crossing the river at a weir between these last two lochs at GR 257235.

5

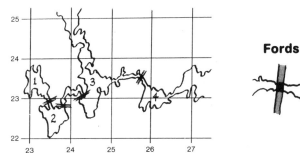

Key to Lochs
1   Loch nan Eilean
2   Loch Roineval
3   Loch Fadagoa
4   Loch Trealaval

Fords

The advice given in the introduction on safety on the moor applies with even more force in this area. Carry compass, map and whistle; wear warm and waterproof clothing; be well shod; take something to eat and drink; and leave clear information behind on where you are going and when you expect to be back.

LOCH NAN EILEAN

Location: **North of the hill Roineval beyond Loch Roineval.**
Grid Reference: **232232**
Area: **52 acres (21 hectares)**

This is an attractive clear-water loch with many bays, promontories and small islands, several of which are easily accessible from the north-west corner of the loch when the water-level is not too high. The large headland to the south of the main body of the loch can be productive.

This loch fishes better in early and late season when the fly-fisher can expect good-quality, light-coloured trout of between eight and ten ounces on average, with much bigger ones always a possibility.

A group of small, **unnamed lochs** lying within three-quarters of a mile of the north-east corner of Loch nan Eilean all contain trout, some producing a good average size of eight ounces or more.

LOCH ROINEVAL

Location: **Lying to the north of the hill Roineval this loch is almost continuous with the shallow south-east end of Loch nan Eilean. The shores are large slabs of rock except for the southern bay, which has a sand and shingle bottom.**
Grid Reference: **235225**
Area: **72 acres (29 hectares)**

The trout rise readily to the fly but are smaller in size and often of poorer quality than those of Loch nan Eilean. However, some very good fish both in size (up to a pound) and quality can be taken from the southern bay.

LOCH A' BHROMA

Location: **To the north-west of the hill Trealaval.**
Grid Reference: **252242**
Area: **30 acres (12 hectares)**

An interesting loch of high banks except on its west side. It fishes better in May and June than at other times. The trout are of good quality, usually red-fleshed, on average about eight ounces, but fish of a pound and over come to the fly, though worm and spinner are more popular.

LOCH NA CISTE

Location:	**About three-quarters of a mile north-north-west of Loch a' Bhroma.**
Grid Reference:	**246253**
Area:	**20 acres (8 hectares)**

Contains trout averaging eight ounces which rise fairly well to the fly.

LOCH MOR AN FHADA MHOIR

Location:	**Lies just north of the hill Fada Mor, to the north-west of Loch na Ciste.**
Grid Reference:	**255257**
Area:	**27 acres (11 hectares)**

This loch is easily fished into deep water from its banks. The fish are mainly small, running to about eight ounces.

The angler who attains this loch has come to the point of no return! The distance back to the Balallan peat road is the same as to the A858 Achmore road.

Do not confuse this loch with Loch an Fhada Bhig which lies just over a mile to the north and which is dealt with on page 56.

LOCH AN DRUNGA

Location:	**A short walk from the east end of Loch a' Bhroma.**
Grid Reference:	**265247**
Area:	**49 acres (20 hectares)**

5

The north side is steep, but the finger-like bays on the south side lie in much flatter ground.

Numerous small trout up to about six ounces come easily to the fly but are of no great quality.

UNNAMED LOCH 1

Approximately one mile north-east of the summit of the hill Trealaval and lying in a steep-sided valley running north-south (GR 273248). After a long moor walk, the angler should be rewarded with trout of around twelve ounces average size.

UNNAMED LOCH 2

Approximately one mile to the east of the summit of the hill Trealaval, lying in a flat area of moor (GR 272240) and easily fished from its banks. Trout run up to eight to ten ounces, but much larger trout are occasionally taken. It is known locally as Loch Cleit a Ghunna.

If returning from these lochs to the river crossing point at GR 257235, the angler who still has the energy to climb to the summit of Trealaval at GR 261238 will be amply rewarded by magnificent all-round views of a landscape of sparkling lochs, hills and moorland.

LOCH FADAGOA (FADAGOTH)

Location:	**To the north and east of the hill Roineval.**
Grid Reference:	**242240**
Area:	**277 acres (112 hectares)**

This is a very extensive area of water over two miles long with an infinite variety of shoreline from rock to deep heather (which last can make walking awkward) and the same variety of fishing situations. Trout average around eight to ten ounces but can run to two pounds and more.

The long bay leading towards Loch Trealaval and the crossing place has beautiful golden trout.

LOCH TREALAVAL

Location:	**To the south of the hill Trealaval.**
Grid Reference:	**270235**
Area:	**370 acres (150 hectares)**

This long and winding loch, the headwater of a salmon and seatrout system, collects its water from Loch Fadagoa to the west and the lochs south of Achmore, through the Lag na Linne (Leig na Linne) to the east, itself draining into Loch nam Faoileag at its eastern end and thence to the sea by way of the Laxay River and Loch Valtos.

The trout size is very similar to that of Loch Fadagoa.

OTHER LOCHS IN THE AREA

LOCH STRANDAVAT (STRANNDAVAT)

Location:	**Half way between the villages of Balallan and Arivruaich (Aribruach) on the A859 road.**
Grid Reference:	**255193**
Area:	**121 acres (49 hectares)**

Trout are fairly plentiful and mostly from six to ten ounces. The best fishing area is from the narrows down towards the road on both sides of the loch, and around the islands. Most of the far side of the narrow section is shallow. The north-west corner is partly overgrown with weeds but during the season the occasional salmon and sea trout can be taken here.

This is a Soval Angling Association loch somewhat separated from the main group to the north.

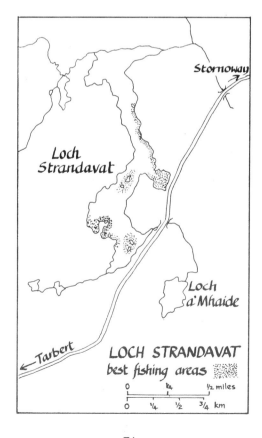

5

LOCH A' MHAIDE

Location: **South-west of the south end of Loch Strandavat and best approached from the A859 Stornoway to Tarbert road.**

Grid Reference: **257180**

Area: **15 acres (6 hectares)**

The east side of this small loch is deeper than the west. Trout of up to a pound will rise to the fly, but the quality has fallen off recently.

Loch an Iar (GR 270178) and **Loch na Muilne** (GR 275177) are two lochs which are easily accessible a mile up the Eishken road from its junction with the A859 just across from the middle of Loch Strandavat. Trout run to about ten ounces, are of good quality, come well to the fly and fight well.

LOCH NA CREIGE FRAOICH

Location: **On the west side of the A857 Stornoway to Tarbert road, about half a mile south of Soval Lodge.**

Grid Reference: **342242**

Area: **22 acres (9 hectares)**

Plenty of trout in good condition up to eight ounces. Fishes well to the fly throughout the season.

Loch an Eilean (Eilein) Liath, a little to the south, is very similar. **Loch na h-Airigh Uir, Loch na Speireig, Loch Eastaper and Dubh Loch Subhal (Shobhail)** to the west and north-west of Loch na Creige Fraoich form a group of lochs set in two steep valleys to the west of the hill Knock More Soval (Cnoc Mor Shobhail) (GR 336250) among which an interesting day can be spent because of the variety of scenery and the different characteristics of the lochs themselves. They all contain small trout, usually less than eight ounces.

LOCH NA CRIADHA

Location:	**Take the peat road, quite suitable for cars, from the A859 at GR 331221 at Laxay, beside a small conifer plantation. Be very careful to close the three gates after passing through. Take the left fork of the peat road after passing Loch Ulapoll.**
Grid Reference:	**318228**
Area:	**25 acres (10 hectares)**

This loch has a stony bottom and wading can be awkward, especially along the east shore. It becomes weedy later in the season, but good well-conditioned trout can be taken all round the loch although the average is only five to six ounces.

Probably the best area is the east side where bigger fish lie, just off the weed beds. One of two pounds was taken on fly there recently, early in the season.

LOCH KEADRASHAL (CEADRAISVAL)

Location:	**Leave your car at Loch na Criadha and walk north for about ten minutes from the peat road end. Aim for the TV mast above Achmore. The loch is not seen until you are on it!**
Grid Reference:	**316238**
Area:	**10 acres (4 hectares)**

This small loch has fished well, especially to flies, in recent years probably because of reseeding schemes in the area. The boulder-strewn bottom makes it difficult to wade, except in a small part of the shallow south-west corner, but it is easily fished from the bank in most places. The trout are of very good quality averaging six to eight ounces but running to twelve ounces and occasionally the pound. Fish tend to rise in concentrated bursts of activity, when the fly-fisher can do well, then suddenly everything switches off, sometimes for hours!

5

LOCH FADA

Location:	**A short walk north of Loch Keadrashal.**
Grid Reference:	**318244**
Area:	**91 acres (37 hectares)**

A big expanse of water, but the banks are easily fishable. Very much a loch for worming or spinning. There is a good head of trout, mainly small but with bigger ones appearing from time to time.

LOCHS IN UIG

Take the A858 road, turning on to the B8011 at Garynahine.

The Allt na Muilne lochs, **Loch nam Fiasgan** (GR 218285), **Loch an Ois Ghuirm** (GR 226278) and **Loch Cleit Stermeis** (GR 232269) are best approached from GR 228297 on the B8011 road, about a mile from the Grimersta river, where an arm of Loch Roag known as Loch Ceann Hulavig (Thulavaig) comes close to the roadside.

This is a better route than the more obvious one half a mile further on at Allt na Muilne where there are numerous fences.

The trout in these lochs are variable in size, and you can expect anything from six ounces to one and a quarter pounds. You may also encounter salmon kelts in Loch an Ois Ghuirm. These should be very carefully returned if taken.

Loch Cleit Steirmeis should not be confused with Loch Cleit Eirmis (GR 242276) which lies further to the east and contains only small dark trout.

LOCH SGAIRE

5

Location: **At the junction of the Bernera road (B8059) and the Uig road (B8011).**
Grid Reference: **197286**
Area: **59 acres (24 hectares)**

The best trout are taken from the Bernera road side of the loch where you can expect trout up to one pound though the average weight is about ten ounces. There is also the possibility of some sea trout during the season.

A pleasant loch to fish which would be ideal from a boat. One may be available from time to time. Apply at Grimersta Lodge.

LOCH SMUAISAVAL

Location:	**North of Loch Sgaire on the east side of the Bernera road but not visible from the road.**
Grid Reference:	**200300**
Area:	**69 acres (28 hectares)**

The loch can be approached from either the Bernera road or the Linshader road. If approaching from the Bernera road cross the moor at a point near the end of the small loch just beyond Loch Sgaire. From the Linshader side walk down by the fence near the cattle-grid.

This loch has excellent quality trout from eight ounces to one and a quarter pounds and when the conditions are favourable fishes best at the north-west end, though big trout of between four and five pounds have been seen rising at the small islands at the south end of the loch. Well worth spending a day's fishing on. Not very suitable for wading and care should be taken if doing so.

LOCH A' PHEALUIR MOR

Location:	**Coming from Stornoway on the B8011 road and having passed through Enaclete (GR 122285) you will find Loch Sandavat on the right of the road. Immediately on the left of the road at the north end of the loch is the entrance to a fank (an enclosure for sheep). Follow the peat road from there down to Loch Croistean, park there, and follow the stream up the glen to the loch.**
Grid Reference:	**097300**
Area:	**67 acres (27 hectares)**

The trout are plentiful, averaging eight ounces, but some reach the pound.

LOCH SGAILLER (SGAILLEIR)

Location:	**Easily accessible, this loch runs alongside the road past the doctor's surgery between Miavaig and Cliff.**
Grid Reference:	**085354**
Area:	**12 acres (5 hectares)**

This loch is underfished yet has yielded trout of an average weight of eight ounces with some reaching the pound or more. Though more often fished with bait, after early spring the fly comes into its own, with Silver Invicta and Grouse and Claret being very effective. The bigger fish seem to be fry feeders; so a lure pattern on the point, especially a fry imitation such as a Polystickle or Robert McHaffie's Storm Fry is worth trying.

LOCH MOR

Location: Turn left at Cliff, as if going down to the beach, then turn immediately sharp left towards a bungalow. Go through the gate (making sure to close it after you) then up a steep winding peat road, taking the right fork. Loch Mor is the second, larger loch on the right.

Grid Reference: 072363

Area: 12 acres (5 hectares)

A splendid loch for beginners and young anglers who need their confidence built up by plenty of practice on many small, free-rising trout.

LOCH A' GHEOIDH

Location: As for Loch Mor, but on reaching the fork on the peat road, take the left fork. Be sure to park well off the road to allow free passage for other vehicles.

Grid Reference: 075350

Area: 12 acres (5 hectares)

The trout are much bigger than those on Loch Mor, but not as plentiful. Worm fishing is successful, but fly-fishing has proved more difficult.

LOCH TRIALAVAT

Location: Take the right fork at the Valtos Outdoor Centre (marked as 'school' on the OS map at GR 087363) and park on the left at the top of the hill.

Grid Reference: 090358

Area: 17 acres (7 hectares)

5

Some years ago over 2000 rainbow trout were released in this loch, growing well and reaching to over three pounds in weight. The resident otters have taken their share, but according to reports some rainbows still remain and are reputed to be very big. If this is so, then they must be unique as a breeding (or very long-lived) rainbow population so far north in the UK.

LOCH LINISH (LINIS)

Location: Take the right fork at the doctor's surgery at Miavaig (at the south end of Loch Sgailler) and follow the road through Uigen. Take the right fork at Reef and follow the road until Loch Linish can be seen on the left down in the glen.

Grid Reference: 113350

Area: 10 acres (4 hectares)

The trout average twelve ounces and are of good quality. The loch fishes best in a warm wind.

Please ask permission at one of the far houses to cross the crofts.

SOUTH LOCHS

Again an appropriately named district. Its wealth of trout fishing has attracted an increasing number of visitors, from those happy to fish the roadside lochs to those who relish the long trek to rarely visited lochs — and those who fish the many waters between these extremes in this peaceful and beautiful place. The entry point to the fishings of South Lochs is the B8060 road at the west end of Balallan (GR 268202).

LOCH OYAVAT (ORAVAT)

Location: **Half a mile south of the village of Shiltenish this small, narrow loch nestles in a valley and is not easily seen from the road.**
Grid Reference: **278187**
Area: **12 acres (5 hectares)**

This loch can yield good quality trout up to eight or more ounces on the fly in the early part of the season, but does not appear to do so well later.

LOCH NA CRAOIBHE

Location: **Half way between the villages of Shiltenish and Habost on the B8060 road to Lemreway.**
Grid Reference: **300182**
Area: **57 acres (23 hectares)**

Ten minutes walk southwards from the road takes you to the north end of the loch. The left bank from this point can be fished with fly, but the best part is the area opposite the island. The bay on the west side opposite the island is also good.

Trout are between eight and ten ounces.

Near the road to the north-west of Loch na Craoibhe is **Loch Dubh** (GR 294192), which is full of small trout. It is an ideal beginners loch. Further along the road on the left is **Loch Mor an Iaruinn**, where the trout disappeared after road-workings affected it. There are signs of recovery, and it may be worth a cast.

6

A short walk to the east of the south end of Loch na Craoibhe is **Loch Clach na h-Iolaire** (GR 305182) which lies below the Clach na h-Iolaire (The Eagle's Rock), a large monolith. This small loch, with its extensive weed beds, has some large trout to well over two pounds, but they are not of good quality.

LOCH NA CISTE and
LOCH CHRAGOL (CHRAGOIL).

Location: South of the village of Habost.
Grid Reference: 320182
Area: 20 acres (8 hectares) and 22 acres (9 hectares)

The best approach is from the cattle grid before you enter Habost. The two lochs are connected by a very short stream (though not according to the latest Ordnance Survey map!) but usually Loch na Ciste is more productive.

The trout, mostly between six and ten ounces, are of good quality and give good sport with fly.

The whole of Loch na Ciste except the bay at the south end, which becomes covered with rushes in mid season, is fishable.

The south side of Loch Chragol is best, where trout are from six to eight ounces and also very good with fly.

Unfortunately, the size of trout in both lochs appears to have fallen off over the past few years, but recovery is always possible.

LOCH AN TARBEIRT

Location: **Take the well-surfaced little road to the right, half-way betwen Kershader and Garyvard, about half a mile past the Kershader war memorial on the B8060 road. You can drive to the side of the loch, but take care not to block access. This road soon becomes a peat road and goes much further into the moor than the OS map shows.**
Grid Reference: **349198**
Area: **17 acres (7 hectares)**

This loch holds good-quality trout of between six and eight ounces and fishes well from all shores, especially the steeper east side.

If you follow the peat road there are several, often weedy, lochs which are worth fishing with small blackish wet flies, small spinners and, especially in the loch at the end of the road, dry flies of various sorts. From Loch an Tarbeirt you can easily walk over to **Loch nan Caor** which, because of reseeding schemes in the area, holds much bigger fish. Loch nan Caor can be more directly reached from the peat road at Garyvard.

LOCH GHOBHAINN

Location:	Take the peat road at Garyvard mentioned above past Loch nam Breac (unnamed) on the right. Loch Ghobhainn is further on, to the left. Take care, as the road is not ideal for the normal car, and always close gates behind you and park off the road.
Grid Reference:	362188
Area:	17 acres (7 hectares)

This loch and **Loch nam Breac** can give an average of eight ounces with the occasional much larger fish. Local and visiting anglers swear by the Black Zulu and Blue Zulu, but Kate McLaren is catching up!

CAVERSTA LOCHAN

Location:	This tiny lochan can be seen on the left alongside the road to Gravir, beside the turn-off for Caversta.
Grid Reference:	368192
Area:	2.5 acres (1 hectare)

It fishes well in March and April when the average is between eight to twelve ounces, with bigger ones about. It becomes impossibly weedy later in the season.

The Caversta river runs near the road here. Seatrout are beginning to run again, after illegal netting ceased, and the small active trout may attract the beginner.

LOCH MOR AN TANGA

Location:	About ten minutes walk to the east of the Caversta side road.
Grid Reference:	377195
Area:	30 acres (12 hectares)

Very seldom fished in recent years, but there are reports of large fish, which do not look like brown trout, being taken — possibly slob trout or seatrout. The exploring angler may find this an interesting loch.

6

LOCH CAOL EISHAL

Location: **Immediately on the left near the turn-off for Cromore and Marvig on the way to Gravir.**
Grid Reference: **379181**
Area: **12 acres (5 hectares)**

Another seldom-fished loch which has produced good bags of eight-ounce trout for those few who have tried it. As it is weedy round the margins and the insect life is considerable it should prove productive to careful fishing.

LOCH CATISVAL

Location: **Take the turn-off to the left for Cromore and Marvig immediately after Loch Caol Eishal, then the right fork to Marvig.**
Grid Reference: **404185**
Area: **54 acres (22 hectares)**

Once a rainbow trout farm, then a rainbow fishery, then holding salmon smolt cages, this loch has been well fed in recent years and the average size of the brown trout has increased to an average of near the pound. It is possible that Co-Chomunn na Pairc will open the loch as a put-and-take rainbow fishery, but nothing has been decided as we go to press.

Boats are available from Mr Donald Maclennan, 19 Marvig.

LOCH CROMORE

Location: **Immediately south of the village of Cromore.**
Grid Reference: **404205**
Area: **49 acres (20 hectares)**

As you enter the village of Cromore over the small bridge the loch is on your right. It is tidal in its lower reaches, and it is possible to catch brown trout, seatrout and slob trout. Even small flounders and lythe have taken the fly here!

A boat is available from Mrs Christina Macleod, 11 Cromore (the house before the bridge).

THE SQUARE LOCH

Location: **This is unnamed on the OS map. It is on the left side, adjacent to the B8060 road to Gravir, about half a mile south of the Cromore/Marvig turn-off.**

Grid Reference: **382169**

Area: **7 acres (3 hectares)**

All areas fish well, the north-east corner being specially recommended. There are considerable midge (chironomid) hatches, and a prolific sedge hatch; so late summer dry fly and emerger patterns can be very effective. Muddlers, Suspender Buzzer, Cul de Canard and wet flies such as Bibio recommended.

LOCH CAOL

Location: **The long loch across the road to the west of the Square Loch.**

Grid Reference: **378166**

Area: **7 acres (3 hectares)**

Affected by roadworks recently, but has recovered. Lots of small fish around the margins, but much larger fish in the middle which respond to long-line and well-sunk fly tactics.

As it is the head loch of the Caversta River, it may have salmon or seatrout, but this has not been proved, though several anglers fishing light have reported being broken by the one that got away!

Do not wade! There are patches of soft mud, and the loch can deepen suddenly.

LOCH CROIS AILEIN

Location: **A large double loch on the east side of the road as you near Gravir. It can be approached either by turning off on to the old road on the left and walking down the bank or by driving past the council houses to the left in Gravir to Crois Ailein Lodge where boats can be hired.**

Grid Reference: **385160**

Area: **37 acres (15 hectares)**

6

A large population of free-rising trout of good quality and ten to twelve-ounce average size, with much larger ones about.

LOCH NAM FAOILEAG

Location: **Between Gravir and Calbost.**
Grid Reference: **400157**
Area: **32 acres (13 hectares)**

Another loch which has benefited from the extra feeding from smolt cages, and the very good-quality trout average round the pound. After storms smashed some cages, the smolts released have been returning as grilse, and some have been caught recently. The loch can be fished all round its shores, but the deeper southern side may hold even bigger fish.

Further along the road to Calbost is **Loch Mirkavat** (GR 410169) which has lots of free-rising trout, difficult to catch, and becomes weeded in June. Beyond Calbost on the right is **Loch na Buaile Duibhe**, in a beautiful location, seldom fished but reputed to have a seatrout run.

LOCH NAN EILEAN and
LOCH TOTAICHEAN AULAIDH (AMHLAIDH)

Location: **West of the Garyvard-Gravir road.**
Grid References: **362175 and 350175**
Area: **60 acres (24 hectares) and 57 acres (23 hectares)**

The peat road from Garyvard takes you to within ten to fifteen minutes of the lochs, but drive and park carefully, closing all gates behind you. The easiest, but not the shortest, walk is from the west end of Glen Gravir (Glenside on the OS map), parking outside the last house, No 15, and walking north or north-west. Take map and compass: returning from Loch nan Eilean to Glen Gravir can sometimes be confusing.

Loch nan Eilean has a big population of high-quality trout around eight ounces, and bigger ones on occasion, which rise freely to the fly. It fishes well all season. The best areas are from the north to midway down the west side, the point on the east side to the north of the numerous small bays, and the bay at the south end.

Small (12s and 14s) dark flies, Haul a Gwynt, Teal and Black and the unfailing Peter Ross have done well.

Loch Totaichean Aulaidh has fish of the same size and quality as Loch nan Eilean, but some very big trout have been taken on the fly, especially in the evenings. A recent evening bag for one fly-fisher was four of over two pounds; four of over one and three-quarters; and four of over a pound.

LOCH DUBH

Location:	**This is unnamed on the OS map. It is on the south side of the road between Lemreway and Orinsay, across the road from Loch Mor na Muilne.**
Grid Reference:	**371123**
Area:	**10 acres (4 hectares)**

Reseedings have improved this loch. The west bank has trout of excellent quality, pounders and larger being common, with smaller trout on the east side. The west side is very dangerous, however, with deep water close in and a high bank behind. Blue Zulu, size 10 (which does well all over South Lochs) is recommended.

There are other lochs to the west of the Gravir to Lemreway road which are well worth exploring.

A boat is available for hire from Mr Murdo Macinnes at Seaview Cottage, 6 Orinsay.

Other recommended lochs in the area are **Loch Bhreacaich**, west of Lemreway, and **Loch Kinneastal** and **Loch Uisge Mhaith Mor (Mor an Uisge Mhaith)** to the north-east.

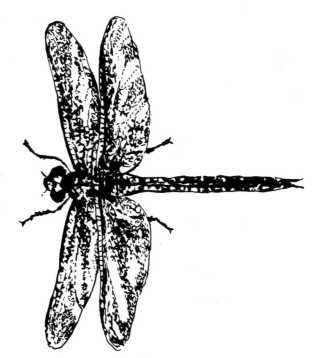

6

WILDLIFE AND THE ANGLER

Trout are not the only inhabitants of the lochs of the Lews nor anglers the only creatures on or near their shores, but some of us may have wondered from time to time when the trout are not rising and the loch for all the world an empty place when and how trout came to our lochs and streams.

We are told that, following the retreat of the ice at the close of the last ice age some 10,000 years ago, the common ancestor of the brown and sea trout, a fish like the latter able to live in both salt and fresh water, ascended our rivers and streams to spawn. Some remained to become brown trout or were trapped in land-locked lochs. Others retained their migratory habit and returned to the sea when not breeding. Other species of fish came after the same manner: salmon, charr, fresh-water eels and three- and ten-spined sticklebacks. Of these, charr and the ten-spined stickleback are the least common although the former are found in more lochs than is generally thought. Occasionally, sea fish enter coastal lochs; thick-lipped grey mullet, for example, occur in Loch Shader near Tolstachaolais and Barvas is renowned for once yielding a sturgeon. I have caught a sea lamprey in Stornoway harbour and it would not be suprising if they were found in the Creed and other rivers and streams. One loch only, Langavat in central Lewis, holds very large cannibal trout called *salmo ferox*, the heaviest of which so far landed weighed, I believe, eleven pounds.

Apart from man, several predators hunt trout. Otters spring to mind in this connection but their preferred prey is the eel, the only fish I have seen them take. I must confess, however, that on one never-to-be-forgotten morning when I was playing a large sea trout on Loch Lacasdail in South Lochs I became aware that an otter also was interested in my fish and was closely following its efforts to escape. Fascinated as I was by otters I had no wish to play one on my fly rod so I chased it away with a stone. Otters have poor eyesight but a keen sense of smell; if an angler is down wind of one he can enjoy, as I have done more than once, an experience denied to most people and quite absorbing enough to divert one's attention from fishing. Other incidents which have effectively put an end for a while to my efforts to catch fish include the swoop of a golden eagle, which I had inadvertently disturbed, over the head of a black-throated diver. The ejaculation and panic dive of the latter were quite unjustified since the eagle continued across the loch but the instinctive reaction was understandable. On another occasion I was walking through thick heather from one part of Loch Borasdale near Carloway intent upon luring one of its beautiful trout to my fly when a black and gold bird rose at my feet and shot round the hillside. It was the first golden oriole I had ever seen and the first for the Outer Hebrides. That was the end of my fishing for that day as I tried to find it again. A third and final example of alien influence occurred one day when I was fishing Loch an Easa Ghil and had half an eye on a skein of geese overhead on migration. To my astonishment a golden eagle stooped out of nowhere through the rear of the flock and caused it to scatter with cries of indignation. The eagle could easily have struck down a goose had it so wished but I guessed it was just teasing the geese and thanked my lucky stars that a salmon hadn't risen to my fly during the incident.

Returning to the subject of predators on trout, one cannot omit mention of that arch pest the feral mink and of the cormorant. The latter takes probably the greatest toll and flies considerable distances inland to satisfy its appetite for trout and smolts. Red-breasted mergansers spend spring and summer bringing up their young beside a freshwater loch and doubtless take a number of trout which I, for one, would not deny them nor the stately heron. It is worth laying down one's rod for a moment if one of these most subtle of fishermen is in the vicinity and learn how to catch fish without disturbing them. They usually nest on our sea cliffs but here and there small heronries are found on islands. One such traditional site on Loch Keose was abandoned when the loch became a popular fishing resort and anglers should always take care not to approach nesting birds of whatever species so close as to put them off the nest. Two species of divers are especially sensitive to such interference, the black- and red-throated divers. The former is very rare and is accorded special protection by law. This handsome bird is found on only a handful of large lochs where it nests on the very shores of islands, whence it can slip unseen into deep water but leaving its eggs or young vulnerable to crows or gulls. Anglers who become aware of the presence of one of these divers between May and August should retreat at once to allow it to return to its nest. The red-throated diver prefers small lochs or tarns for breeding where the sight of one ought to divert the humane angler to another part of the moor. It usually feeds in the sea and the summer visitor will often hear its duck-like cackle overhead as it flies to and from the sea.

But the fish-eating bird par excellence is surely the osprey. In May a few of these magnificent fishers migrate through the Hebrides on their way from Africa to breed in Scandinavia and can be observed by the fortunate at any estuary or even over some of our lochs. The late William Matheson once had the enviable experience of sharing Loch Mhic Leoid with a fishing osprey. No one can be in any doubt of an osprey's identity if he sees a large eagle-like bird splash down into a loch and disappear momentarily in the cascade of water thrown up by the impact and he could be forgiven for relaxing his attention to the business of catching fish for himself; but the quickest way to end a perfect friendship is to tell an angler there is an osprey just as a trout rises to his fly.

Some birds which may be seen on loch or stream are not in competition with the angler. A pair of common sandpipers inhabit most lochs in summer and call attention to themselves as they flit from shore to shore on intermittently whirring wings and with a shrill, piping call. The black and white dipper is found on most of our larger streams, where it bounces up and down on stones from which it dives and pursues small creatures on the bottom. The rippling song of the wren, surprisingly loud for such a tiny bird, is a common feature of many a loch and river side but the graceful arctic and common terns which used to nest by quite a few Lewis lochs seem to be dying out, probably owing to the depredations of the ubiquitous mink. The isolated colonies of greylag geese are also a thing of the past for the same reason although interference by man burning the heather on their nesting islands and stealing eggs and young is also a factor.

So much for the feathered companions of the trout fisherman. A winged creature of a very different sort which makes its presence felt upon him in no uncertain manner is known to entomologists as *culicoides impunctatus* and to anglers and peat cutters as the : . . midge. The eggs, which are laid in water, take a year to grow into pupae and are devoured by trout as they rise to the surface — but millions survive to torment us.

The most spectacular insects we are likely to come across are the dragon- and damsel-flies of which *aeshna juncea* and *ischnura elegans* are the commonest. Their colourful bodies and wings and lightning movements are unlike anything else around. The fly fisherman has, of course, a vested interest in the insect food of his quarry and should consult an appropriate book for further information on this abstruse subject.

The vegetation on which this insect life is dependent is also of concern and not only when it interferes with our casting. With the exception of a very few coastal lochs the vegetation is scarce and confined to a small number of species. Those which attract the attention are the white water lily, water lobelia and bogbean. On one small loch in the Eishken estate a beautiful red water lily is found but it was probably introduced. Most anglers are, however, fishing in water too deep for these colourful plants and will come across only the floating maroon and green oval leaves of the pond weeds. At lunch time and for a rest they may land on an island in the loch, always careful not to disturb nesting birds, and, if they have eyes to see, admire the luxuriance of the vegetation in comparison with that of the surrounding moorland. No fire nor omnivorous sheep has destroyed the thick cover of dwarf willow, aspen, rowan, juniper, crowberry and royal fern.

All things considered the angler in Lewis has a great deal for which to be thankful and the more observant he is the more his gratitude. There is an almost infinite variety of fishable water and our unpredictable climate ensures equally variable conditions, absence of wind seldom one of them. A wise man of the past, Duncan Macaulay of Breasclete, known as the Moortrotter, has written about the lochs of Lewis that "The prevailing wind is from the south-west. The waves of countless ages, moving the waters to the north-east and beating against the north-east shores have dissolved the soil and pounded the stone and rock. The returning undercurrents have carried the sands at the rate of one inch per annum, more or less, to the south-western shores. You may thus expect to find shallow sandy beaches on the south-western shores and a deep, rock bound or boulder-strewn shore in the north-east. Here is where the trout usually live. The action of wind and wave bring a harvest of dead and dying flies. There is shade in the shadow of the rocks and boulders, and the eddying waters among the rocks stir up, and create the little currents which the trout delight to be in.''

10 Barony Square   *Peter Cunningham*
Stornoway
12 April 1985

References

CAMPBELL. R.N., Ferox Trout & Char in Scottish Lochs. J. Fish Biol. (1979) 14.

CUNNINGHAM. P., A Hebridean Naturalist. Acair. 1979.

SMITH. W. ANDERSON, Lewsiana. Dalby, Isbister & Co. 1875.

WATERSTON. A.R. et al. The Inland Waters of the Outer Hebrides. Proc. Roy. Soc. Edin. 77B. 1979.

CONSERVATION OF BROWN TROUT IN LEWIS AND HARRIS

There are so many lochs containing so many brown trout in Lewis and Harris that it would be easy to think that there are no threats to them. We, as anglers, must be vigilant, and identify any threats at an early stage. We must then be prepared to take whatever steps are appropriate to avoid damage to our brown trout populations.

The wild brown trout became established in Scotland 10,000 years ago, when sea trout invaded the rivers after the last ice age. There is scientific evidence from Ireland that proves that there are several genetically distinct varieties of brown trout. As yet, there has been no similar work done in Scotland, but there is undoubtedly a similar degree of variation to be found here too. This genetic variety must be preserved.

Brown trout spawn in small burns, and also within lochs when conditions are suitable. Protection of the entire habitat ensures protection of the species. The possible sources of damage in Lewis and Harris include pollution, drainage, afforestation, introduced fish, other introduced species.

Nutrient input is the most obvious pollution problem. The majority of the lochs in Lewis and Harris have a very low nutrient level. Additional nutrient input can come from fish cages (food & faeces), reseeded areas of moorland and other wastes (septic tanks etc.). Initially, an extra input of nutrients can quite dramatically improve the quality of the brown trout population due to the increase in food production. There comes a point, however, when the loch can no longer cope with the high nutrient levels. At this stage, algal blooms can occur, which can lead to large fish kills caused by oxygen deprivation.

Drainage in loch catchments, often associated with afforestation, can cause damage to valuable spawning areas. In general, the drains enable more particulate material to enter the streams, which can destroy the spawning beds by siltification. The increased rate of run-off from the land causes spates to occur at a faster rate than before. Such 'flash floods" can wash away gravel beds used for spawning, depositing them elsewhere in unsuitable locations.

Stocking lochs with brown trout has been done in the past, with mixed success, and will certainly be done in the future. Indiscriminate supplementary stocking can interfere with the natural population, causing more harm than good. In all stocking programmes, only trout of the same genetic character as the natural population should be used. As each and every loch is different, and has different requirements, it is important to seek expert advice in advance of any such programmes.

Stocking with rainbow trout has become very popular nationally. These fish are easy to rear, fast growing and easy to catch. Whilst there are no self-sustaining populations of rainbow trout in Britain to date (due to spawning failure), overstocking of rainbow trout can lead to rainbows outcompeting the wild brown trout for food. Wild brown trout populations must be preserved, and on no account should put-and-take rainbow fisheries compromise wild brown trout populations.

There are no native species of coarse fish in Lewis and Harris. There is a minority of anglers who would like to see the introduction of coarse species such as pike. Should this occur and a pike population become established, it could mean disaster for the wild brown trout populations. There are no laws against this at present, but it is of paramount importance that no such introductions take place. For anybody even to contemplate such an introduction would be highly irresponsible.

To introduce any animals to an environment where they do not occur naturally is a dangerous practice. The Western Isles ecosystem has developed over the centuries without the presence of many species that cannot get here because of the Minch. In effect, the ecosystem has been very finely tuned over the years. The artificial introduction of any new species to this finely balanced system is asking for trouble. Seemingly harmless species can disrupt food chains and indirectly damage natural populations. There have been several attempts in recent years to introduce frogs to the islands, at least two of which seem to have been successful (Great Bernera and Marybank). We simply cannot predict with accuracy the consequences of such introductions to our ecosystem. Past experience tells us that, more often than not, introducing non-native species to fragile ecosystems leads to harmful effects, and should therefore be avoided at all costs.

As anglers, we are in a position to see and experience our environment to a higher degree than many of our fellow people. We have a responsibility to look after that environment, to ensure that our populations of wild brown trout are protected. This will give us our continued enjoyment of the sport of brown trout fishing, and make sure that it is still available for anglers in the future.

22 Gress   *David Maclennan*
Isle of Lewis
22 February 1993

INDEX

A

Loch Achmore 54
Loch Airigh na Ceardaich 65
Loch Airigh nan Gleann 47
Loch Airigh na Lic 45
Loch Airigh Mhic Fhionnlaidh Duibh . . 39
Loch Airigh Riabhach 41
Loch Airigh Seibh 37
Loch Airigh an Sgairbh 48
Loch Airigh nan Sloc 52
Loch na h-Airigh Uir 72
Loch Almaistean 35
Loch Ard Airigh a' Ghille Ruaidh 52
Loch Aoraidh 31

B

Loch Bacavat GR502442 18
Loch Bacavat GR398552 26
Loch Bacavat GR365450 31
Loch Baravat GR462596 23
Loch Baravat GR155355 60
Loch Beag a' Chocair 46
Loch Beag Cnoc a' Choilich 41
Loch Beag na Craoibhe 42
Loch Beag Eileavat 20
Loch Beag a' Ghrianain 48
Loch Bealach na Sgail 35
Loch a' Bhaile GR255474 33
Loch a' Bhaile GR197385 36
Loch Bharavat 38
Loch Bhreachaich 85
Loch a' Bhroma 68
Loch a' Bhuna 44
Loch Borasdale 35
Loch nam Breac GR282370 39
Loch nam Breac GR357193 81
Loch Breaclete 60
Loch Breivat 33
Loch Breugach 42
Loch Bruthadail 32
Loch na Buaile Duibhe 84

C

Loch Caol 83
Loch Caol Eishal 82
Loch nan Caor 80
Loch nan Caorach 39
Loch Catisval 82
Caversta Lochan 81
Loch Ceann Allavat 39
Loch na Ceannamhoir 60
Loch Chearasaidh 24
Loch Chragol 80
Loch na Ciste GR246253 69
Loch na Ciste GR320182 80
Loch Clach na h-Iolaire 79
Loch nan Cleitichean 37
Loch Cleit Stermeis 75
Loch Cliasam Creag 35
Loch na Cloich 20
Loch nan Cnamh 52
Loch na Craoibhaig 62
Loch na Craoibhe GR300277 55
Loch na Craoibhe GR300182 79
Loch na Creige Fraoich 72
Loch na Creige Guirme 56
Loch na Criadha 73
Loch na Croibhe 65
Loch Crois Ailein 83
Loch Cromore 82
Loch Cuthaig 66

D

Loch an Daimh 56
Loch Dhomhnuill Bhig 66
Loch Dibadale 23
Loch Diridean 20
Loch Druim nan Sgorach 44
Loch an Drunga 69
Loch Dubh GR294192 79
Loch Dubh GR371123 85
Dubh Loch Subhal 72
Loch an Duin GR394543 26
Loch an Duin GR188408 35
Loch an Duna 33

E

Loch Eastaper 72
Loch Eilaster 36
Loch nan Eilean GR333305 44
Loch nan Eilean GR232232 68
Loch nan Eilean GR362175 84
Loch an Eilean Chubhraidh 56
Loch an Eilean Liath 72
Loch an Eilein 17

F

Loch Fada 73
Loch Fada Caol 16
Loch Fadagoa 70
Loch na Faing 14
Loch nam Falcag 55
Loch Faoileag 43
Loch nam Faoileag 84
Loch Fasgro 34
Loch an Fhada Bhig 56
Loch an Fhraoich 39
Loch nam Fiasgan 75
Loch Fionnacleit 35
Loch Foid 55
Loch Foisnavat 14
Loch na Fola 16

G

Loch na Gainmhich 56
Loch nan Geadh GR484464 18
Loch nan Geadh GR205363 53
Loch Geal 59
Loch nan Geadraisean 61
Loch a' Ghainmhich 15
Loch a' Gheoidh 77
Loch Ghobhainn 81
Loch Gobhlach 62
Loch Gobhlaich 56
Loch Gress 14
Loch Grinavat 33
Loch Gunna 15

H

Lower Loch Hatravat 27
Upper Loch Hatravat 27
Lochan Hatravat 28

I

Loch an Iar 72
Loch Ibheir 66
Loch Innseag 51
Loch Ionadagro 19
Loch Ionail 59
Loch Iosal a' Bhruic 55

K

Loch Keadrashal 73
Loch Keartavat 27
Loch Keose 57
Loch Kinneastal 85
Kirkibost Lochs 62

L

Loch Langavat GR525545 21
Loch Langavat GR215440 34
Loch Langavat GR223218—155130 . . 63
Loch Laxavat 37
Loch nan Leac GR430485 13
Loch nan Leac GR445458 16
Loch a' Leadharain 46
Loch Leiniscal 43
Loch Leisavat 25
Loch Linish 78
Loch Lochavat 56

M

Loch Maravat 26
Loch a' Mhaide GR277225 65
Loch a' Mhaide GR257180 72
Loch Mirkavat 84
Loch na Moine 52
Loch Mor GR495543 29
Loch Mor GR072363 77
Loch Mor a' Chocair 46
Loch Mor a' Chrotaich 49
Loch Mor Eileavat 20
Loch Mor an Fhada Mhoir 69
Loch Mor a' Ghoba 19
Loch Mor a' Ghrianain GR265377 . . . 37
Loch Mor a' Ghrianain GR404308 . . . 48
Loch Mor an Iaruinn 79
Loch Mor an Stairr 50
Loch Mor an Tanga 81
Loch na Muilne GR205378 36
Loch na Muilne GR168365 61
Loch na Muilne GR148397 61
Loch na Muilne GR275177 72

O

Loch an Ois Ghuirm 75
Loch Orasay 50
Loch Ordais 33
Loch Oyavat 79

P

Loch a' Phealuir Mor 76

R

Loch nan Ramh 54
Loch Raoinavat 34
Loch Roineval 68
Loch Ruiglavat 25
Loch Ruisavat 24
Loch Rumsagro 24

S

Loch Scarrasdale 19
Loch Sgailler 76
Loch Sgaire 75
Loch an Sgath 67
Lochan a' Sgeil 16
Loch Sgeireach na Creige Brist 22
Loch Sgeireach Mor 18
Loch nan Sgiath 43
Loch Skapraid 56
Loch Sminig 27
Loch Smuaisaval 76
Loch Spealdravat Mor 32
Loch Speireag 44
Loch na Speireig 72
The Square Loch 83
Loch Strandavat 71

T

Loch Tana GR492546 28
Loch Tana GR275280 56
Loch an Tarbeirt 80
Loch Thota Bridein 53
Loch an Tobair 16
Loch an Tomain 67
Loch Tom an Fheidh 51
Loch Totaichean Aulaidh 84
Loch Trealaval 70
Loch Trialavat 77
Loch an Tuim GR425435 15
Loch an Tuim GR255358 38

U

Loch Uisge Mhaith Mor 85
Loch Uisg' an t-Soluis 41
Loch Ullavat a' Clith 17
Loch Ullavat a' Deas 17
Loch Uraval 52
Loch Urrahag 32

V

Lochan Vataleois 21
Loch Vatandip 46

Unnamed Lochs

GR481468 18
GR501468 19
GR525528 22
GR366300 43
GR370305 43
GR400300 49
GR374283 52

GR287268 55
GR180356 62
GR236238 68
GR238238 68
GR235237 68
GR273248 69
GR272240 70

The Editors wish particulary to thank the following for their contributions

Dr J A Barker, Gravir

Mr John Drummond, Ness

Mr John Ingram, Ness

Mr Mackay Irvine, Pitlochry

Mr Alasdair Macdonald, Grimshader

Mr Kenneth Maciver, Stornoway, Bernera and Edinburgh

Mr Norman Mackenzie, Keose

Mr David Maclennan, Gress

Mr John M Macleod, Balallan

Mr Norman Macsween, Scalpay and Inverness

Dr Boyd Peters, South Lochs and Uig

Mr Dave Smith, Uig

Dr W M Speirs, Laxdale

The Publisher wishes additionally to thank

Roddy J Macleod for the sketch map on page 67

Colin Tucker for all other sketch maps

Alison Young for all other line drawings

Eddie Young for the photograph on page 61

Roddy J Macleod for all other monochrome photographs

David Maclennan for the photograph on the back cover

Angus Smith Photographic, Stornoway, from whom prints are available,
for all other colour photographs

Peter Cunningham and David Maclennan for their articles

Nevisprint Ltd, Fort William, for the colour printing

and

The Editors for their industry and enthusiasm